CW00518305

Tangled up in Blue

Blue Labour and the Struggle for Labour's Soul

Rowenna Davis

Foreword by Steve Richards

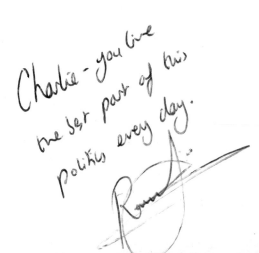

Charlie - you live the best part of this politics every day.

Published in 2011 by
Ruskin Publishing Limited
77 Beak Street
London
W1F 9DB

10 9 8 7 6 5 4 3 2 1

Copyright ©
Rowenna Davis 2011

Rowenna Davis has asserted her right under the Copyright,
Designs and Patents Act 1988 to be identified as the
author of this work. All rights reserved. No part of this
publication may be reproduced, stored in a retrieval system
or transmitted in any form, or by any means (electronic,
mechanical, or otherwise) without the prior written
permission of both the copyright owner and the publisher.

A CIP catalogue record for this book
is available from the British Library.

ISBN 978-1-780-72-068-5

Printed and bound by CPI Group (UK) Ltd, Croydon, CR0 4YY

Contents

Interviewees

Ed Miliband
David Miliband
Maurice Glasman
Catherine Glasman
Stewart Wood
Patrick Diamond
James Purnell
Phillip Blond
Jon Cruddas
Marc Stears
Jonathan Rutherford
Stuart White
Anthony Painter
Jon Wilson
Marcus Roberts
Will Straw
Sunder Katwala
Neil Jameson
Jonathan Cox
Sophie Stephens
Diane Abbott
Jonathan Courouble
Nick Pecorelli
Blair McDougall
Duncan Weldon
Patrick Macfarlane

These interviews were all conducted by audio. Their quotes are taken straight from transcripts, and are reproduced here with minimum editing.

Acknowledgements

This book would not have been possible without the loving and tested support of close friends. Thanks particularly to Neela Doležalova, Jonangelo Molinari, Nigel Mountford and Sam Fenton-Whittet who are always there and my shadow, Renie Anjeh, who makes more insightful contributions at fifteen than most people do at thirty. Thanks also to Sunny Hundal of Liberal Conspiracy, who has always made me the best I can be. Apologies to all the staff at Del Aziz in Bermondsey that this wasn't a novel – I still greatly appreciate the coffee. Thanks also to Mum and Dad – you got Bob Dylan in the title in the end. Thanks to friends at the *Guardian* – particularly Randeep Ramesh, Jonathan Haynes and Aditya Chakrabortty. A special thanks to the support of the wonderful transcriber Vanessa Woodley and the patience of her little girl. Two special mentions – this book wouldn't have been here without the stubborn insistence of Derek Draper that this could be done in a summer, or the phenomenal Steve Richards, who has acted as a patient and wise mentor throughout the entire project. Finally, I would like to thank all my interviewees for the generosity of their time, particularly Maurice. This book is possible because of your openness. I hope you enjoy the story.

Foreword

During the early summer of 2011 a think tank hosted a seminar for some political journalists at Westminster. The guest was Blue Labour's leading pioneer, Maurice Glasman. I almost did not bother to turn up. It was a busy day for politics and all my instincts made me wary of Blue Labour even though I knew nothing about it. Based largely on the name I had assumed it was a derivative, backward looking, defensive and a naively shapeless political project vaguely associated with "community", one of the more conveniently flexible terms in British politics. This was a lunchtime seminar and I was very tempted by a quick coffee in the House of Commons canteen instead of what I feared would be two hours of vague banalities.

I am pleased I resisted the temptation and went to the seminar. After hearing Glasman for an exhilarating two hours extemporising on Blue Labour and responding to questions from senior journalists from across the political spectrum with verve and wit I realised he was on to something and we in the media would soon be on to him. As if from nowhere an important political figure had exploded on to the political stage. Apart from the stimulating, unpredictable and yet authoritative projection of ideas here was someone who had studied Groucho Marx as well as Karl, a committed academic with a glorious sense of the ridiculous.

The importance of what Glasman had to say is partly determined by context. Within days of securing the leadership in the autumn of 2010 Ed Miliband declared that the New Labour era was over. The declaration sparked controversy fuelled largely by some of the early pioneers of New Labour. The pioneers were railing against the inevitable. After a long period of power new leaders always seek to mark a divide with the recent past.

There is a familiar pattern. After the Conservatives' eighteen years of continuous rule their new leader, William Hague, made the need to "move on" the theme of his first party conference speech in the autumn of 1997. Beyond wearing a baseball cap and attending the Notting Hill carnival Hague failed to move very far and fought the 2001 election with policies that were similar to those that his party had espoused four years earlier. After Labour lost in 1979 the party's attempts to move on led to civil war and a formal schism, providing infinite space for the ideologically confident leadership of Margaret Thatcher. In both cases it took more than a decade for the defeated parties to form at least partially coherent programmes that also attracted a wider range of voters. As far as the Conservatives were concerned their attempts to move on were not appealing enough to secure them an overall majority in the 2010 election.

Declaring with cathartic resolution that an era has ended is both necessary and easy after an election defeat. Mapping out what follows is much more nightmarishly challenging. So what next for a Labour party that was more or less ruled by two individuals, Tony Blair and Gordon Brown from 1994? Where will the fresh thinking come from and who will be the thinkers?

Blue Labour has surfaced as the most attention-grabbing source of ideas and fresh thinking on the centre left. Occasionally it commands the front pages. Glasman can fill a hall and is heard with respect when senior political journalists gather to hear his thoughts. Ed Miliband pays intense attention and so does his elder brother, David. The range of those who at least are engaging with Glasman is remarkably wide as are those who are opposed to him, two conflicting coalitions that almost serve a constructive purpose. They nearly wipe away the old brutally destructive divide within Labour of "Blairites" and "Brownites".

There are many causes for surprise that Blue Labour has made significant waves. My original wary instincts to head for a canteen rather than a seminar are not without some foundation. The title is imitative, deploying the same counter intuitive device that made Red Toryism fashionable in the early years of David Cameron's leadership. At least Red Tory was original. Indeed we learn from this revelatory book that the pioneering Red Tory, Phillip Blond, is close to Glasman. The two are friends and Glasman looked on with awe-struck alarm as Blond appeared to be singing some of Labour's more melodious tunes on behalf of the Conservatives. Partly Blue Labour is a direct response to the Red Tory. Imitative projects are usually superficial and tend to flounder pathetically.

The nature of this imitation also conveys a defensiveness that echoes the worst of New Labour. The title Blue Labour implies that Labour can only win by being Conservative, a view that occasionally permeated Blairite thinking as Labour's election winner clung tamely to his big tent of contradictory supporters. No party can blur its boundaries to such an extent that it loses distinctiveness altogether for the obvious reason that it ceases to mean anything at all.

But Glasman is not inclined to blur. His forensic ebullience suggests there is more to Blue Labour than the label suggests. Such is the authenticity of his public voice there is not a hint of political theft from other sources. The defensive, imitative echoes are misleading and explain partly why Blue Labour is so determinedly misunderstood by its coalition of dismissive critics.

As far as Blue Labour has a recognisably coherent agenda it is a radical and daring one. It is not a return to the 1950s, nor is it anti-state, anti-women, anti-immigrants. As Glasman insists the nearest model for Blue Labour in terms of government is Germany, with its more responsible and accountable regional banks, collaborative industrial culture and diverse forms of ownership in the private and public sectors. Ownership is a key interest for Blue Labour and even if analysis and policy solutions are sometimes imprecise it leaps on to fertile terrain. Ownership became a defining theme in 1945 and again after 1979 yet rarely attracts much political attention. Co-operatives, mutuals, the so-called John Lewis model do not work in every instance as senior figures in John Lewis have made clear to indiscriminately admiring politicians, but they represent an alternative form of empowerment for employees and users than the chimera of "choice" that has dominated the narrow debate in British politics for more than a decade. Other key Blue Labour themes such as community, family, being pro-business and yet resolutely hostile to the deregulated financial markets form a coherent set of inter-connected policy areas. Blue Labour speaks to the fashionable politics of responsibility and involvement, a sense of who we are and where we are from. To some extent it also enables Miliband to mount a critique of markets without being labelled "Red Ed". No wonder he is interested.

In British politics ideas rarely flourish without compelling advocates. Glasman has the potential to be a political star, a rare shining light amongst a breed of politicians conditioned to be safely dull. Viewed solely in terms of performance Glasman's instinctive ability to sprinkle wit, mischief and a range of ideas in a speech comes close to the charisma of a previous generation of politicians, when communication extended beyond the art of the soundbite and short interview.

No one can accuse Glasman of mastering modern news management. From his position as a political novice he displays spectacular naivety, a reason why the headlines he generates tend to be destructively controversial. In politics there is such a thing as bad publicity and he attracts it. Yet in spite of himself he has also shown political dexterity, forming close relationships with both Miliband brothers, an almost impossible feat, and attracting an alliance of admirers that defies all familiar political categorisation. Ed Miliband, David Miliband, James Purnell, Jon Cruddas and even some of those who work as advisers for David Cameron are all in varying degrees fans of Glasman and have been influenced by his ideas.

Glasman is also a populist, an unusual gift in an academic. Football is a guide as much as Hayek, one of his favourite economists and one normally more associated with the right. Glasman suggests that Blue Labour turns to Barcelona,

Spain's footballing giants for inspiration, rather than Manchester United. Barcelona is part of the community and on its website states emphatically that in its range of responsibilities is "more than a club". Manchester United is owned by a wealthy family that lives in the United States. Lurking in these accessible comparisons is a celebration of success, including commercial success, but within clearly defined moral boundaries. As a transition to Hayek the glories of Barcelona FC are not a bad route to take.

Blue Labour's flaws are more to do with the limits of what it has to offer so far rather than in its headline-,grabbing populism. Like many thinkers on the edge of politics they avoid some of the basic policy areas that decide elections in Britain. Glasman argues that the state has a role but other agencies have important functions too. It is on those other agencies that he chooses to focus. In doing so he develops important arguments, but makes them when Labour has yet to win even a basic one about the state as a benevolent force rather than a sinister, wasteful one. It is a little too easy to move on and declare that the state has a role to play and leave it at that, not least when the alternative is sometimes vague. As with Cameron's Big Society it is not always clear which binding agencies will bring communities together as an alternative to the state and to whom they will be accountable. Similarly Glasman's call for a rebalancing of the British economy, away from its fragile dependence on financial services, is well made. How the rebalancing is accomplished is more challenging than making the assertion that a transformation is required.

Still the work of re-thinking economic policy, the role of government and other agencies is fundamental to the strange demands of opposition. As Nigel Lawson once astutely observed, the party that wins the battle of ideas wins elections. Glasman's vibrant presence plays at least a part in offering ideological armoury that is a prerequisite to electoral success.

The degree to which he does so is illustrated by making a comparison with the fate of the leading Red Tory, Phillip Blond. At first while the Conservative leadership was in opposition and claiming to be on the progressive side of British politics Blond appeared to be a figure of considerable significance. Cameron attended the launch of Blond's think tank. Blond was asked to help write some of Cameron's speeches. But quickly he became relatively isolated in the Conservative party. While he still has qualified admirers in Cameron's entourage contact is limited and he operates in something of a political vacuum, one in which he hopes might be partially filled by interest from the Labour leadership. Although viewed with great scepticism by some senior figures in the shadow cabinet, already Glasman is in a more influential position within his party. Miliband made him a peer shortly after becoming leader and so with the wave of a wand an academic has a political platform for life. The base is nowhere near as useful as a seat in the Commons and inevitably places a limit on political ambition, but a forum and a position are there for a compelling personality to build upon. Glasman's links with key players in Labour go well beyond Cameron's limited interest in Blond. Glasman's contacts are deep and wide.

This is the narrative of an idea, its extraordinary leading advocate and the impact on two brothers who were doomed to fight each other in a leadership contest. The debate on the future of the Labour party, and the unresolved one in relation to Cameron's early attempts to update Conservatism, require much sharper definition. It is time the hidden story was told.

Steve Richards

Introduction

Maurice Glasman couldn't sleep. On a freezing night in January 2009, he was pacing around his living room that was packed with overflowing cardboard boxes. Restlessly rolling up, he was chain smoking and talking heatedly to his wife, Catherine. The disordered room was crammed with relics from his childhood; ragged exercise books, photographs and dusty trinkets his mother could never bring herself to throw out. Now she was gone. After a deteriorating illness, Rivie Glasman had finally passed away.

Up a set of stairs littered with unlaced shoes and felt tip pens, Glasman's four children lay asleep above their parents. All in one room, their mattresses lay row to row on the floor. A little-known academic, Glasman didn't bring in much money. It was an anxious time for everyone. The country was still reverberating with the fall-out of the financial crisis that began just a few months before. The consequences of Lehman Brothers' collapse were still rippling through the high streets. Small independent shops in Glasman's bohemian neighbourhood were waiting to see what would happen.

In Glasman's mind, his mother's death seemed disturbingly connected with the crisis gripping the country. Rivie had brought him up with a fiery love of family, community and aspiration. Most significantly, she had brought him up to be Labour. Glasman had grown frustrated with the party's inability to connect with those like her. Now his mother's party was in the process of bailing out the richest members of society at the expense of working people. It wasn't just a regressive transfer of wealth; it was a betrayal of his mother's values. Gordon Brown would lose the election, and her party would fall from power. If this was a financial crisis, it was also an emotional one.

It was in this intensely personal moment in his living room, speaking to his wife late that night, that Glasman first used the term "Blue Labour". When Glasman and Catherine look back, it's obvious that this was nothing less than a shared moment of revelation:

GLASMAN: Mum was very strong for people, strong for family … I was just going through what she was into, she was strong for ethics, for being honest, she was really with the poor people my Mum, she was with the naughty ones, what does it mean, she was strong for Labour, she was strong for Jewish things, what does it mean, what does it mean to run towards the grief and honour her? And it came in a horrendous clarity that I just turned to you and said "Blue Labour".

CATHERINE: Yes, it just fitted…

GLASMAN   Blue Labour, Blue was for the mood, my Mum, you wouldn't describe my mother as happy, I have a much happier disposition than my mother she used to find my

perkiness somewhat superficial at times. Then I said Blue
Labour and you went –

CATHERINE: That's perfect, and everything, yes, she was
Orthodox but she was very modern at the same time. She
was completely up to date, watched television, she was
completely with it as well as being very traditional in many
ways.

GLASMAN: Then I remember saying this will change
everything.

CATHERINE: It felt like a magic key.

GLASMAN: … I said this can really work, but it can only work
if I completely commit myself to it, and we agreed.

CATHERINE: We shook hands.

GLASMAN: This will be a big change, I said.

* * *

Barely a year after Blue Labour hit the public stage, it was
pronounced "dead" in political circles. But after a frantic
summer that saw the brand sink in a media storm, the leader
of the Labour party calmly insisted its core ideas remained
undamaged. Sitting in his office in Portcullis House in
Westminster, Ed Miliband spoke warmly about Blue Labour
and its proponents. He may not publicly attach himself to
the label, but he is unashamedly enthusiastic about the ideas
and language that underpin it:

> I think that actually [it's] ahead of its time in a way Blue
> Labour was saying to us look you have to think about the
> values that your society operates under, it's not just always
> about you know how can you get a bit more money for the

health service, or getting more money into education, it's also about something bigger and because it's harder to define, I think it really matters, and this important point which… that the institutions we have and the way they are run speak to a set of values.

The Labour leader went on:

Blue Labour directs you to thinking actually people's relationships really matter and they really enforce the society that you have got and therefore what kind of economy that we have and the way people make money you know, life isn't just about earning and owning, what about your family and the time you have with your family, I think that is very important.

The same day that Ed Miliband was speaking in early September 2011, his brother David Miliband also agreed to be interviewed for this book. It was almost exactly a year since he had lost the leadership election to his younger brother, and the feelings were still raw. Throughout the campaign the media had relished the chance to portray the brothers as politically and personally divided. Ed Miliband was portrayed as the representative of the Brownite faction of the party on the side of the state whilst David Miliband was caricatured as the Blairite champion of the market. So obsessed with finding divisions, the media missed a crucial new overlap of ideas that continues to grow to this day. When asked what lessons the party could take from a set of seminars widely associated with the founding of Blue Labour ideas – David Miliband offers an uncanny echo of his brother:

> The founding insight that significant relationships can counter the power of the market and the state is important... We shouldn't lose the fundamental insight that globalisation and social change can corrode relationships of trust. Politics is about rebuilding those relationships.

Although neither of the Milibands would publicly subscribe to the label, the ideas that Blue Labour discusses are fast becoming a central pillar in the post-Blair-Brown party. After three terms in office, there is a consensus that the state alone cannot solve all of the nation's problems, and the market can't be left to its own devices. It's the third pillar – one that centres on community, relationships and civil society – that is now gaining greater significance. It is Blue Labour's assertion that this is the pillar the party forgot when it was in office, and it is the strand that will have to be reclaimed if Labour is to renew itself and rebuild the trust necessary to win back power.

Others have already got it. David Cameron's commitment to the Big Society agenda is an acknowledgement that this agenda is at least worth fighting for. Writers like David Brooks in *The Social Animal* and Drew Westen in *The Political Brain* have highlighted the importance of emotional connection and psychology in politics. Barack Obama's victorious election campaign in the United States demonstrated what anyone who uses social media has known for a long time – that relationships, emotional connection and participation are now expected much more widely across modern life. In this sense, Blue Labour is only catching up with what Facebook users and the corporate sector already know.

But Blue Labour ideas are not just about acknowledging

the need to embrace something new; they are also about reaffirming something old. Calling for a return to a particular kind of small "c" conservatism, proponents believe that part of reconnecting with people involves recognising that for significant sections of our society, life has not got better with time. Progress is not automatic and change is not always welcome. Globalisation can be terrifying as well as exciting. Blue Labour argues that the party's failure to recognise this helps explain why they have lost 4.5 million working-class voters since 1997, compared to 1.5 million middle-class voters over the same period. Proponents of this analysis believe that reconnecting with the party's traditional base requires Labour to rediscover certain conservative values – whether you call those faith, family and flag or community, responsibility and belonging.

This is the story of how the ideas and actors of Blue Labour sparked an internal debate within the party that gained influence and played an understated part of the leadership battle between the two brothers. Lord Glasman, the founding father of Blue Labour, was little more than an obscure and rather scruffy academic living in an overcrowded flat in Hackney two years ago. On the basis of little more than a few trusted introductions, he quickly came to have a significant and widely underestimated influence on the Labour party. This book will explain how Glasman, a respected thinker, added key policies to Labour's 2010 manifesto, including commitments to the living wage, community land trusts and mutualisation. A self-trained speechwriter, the first address he ever wrote – for the then prime minister Gordon Brown – helped Labour jump 6% in the polls just three days before the general election.

Tangled up in Blue will go on to follow Glasman through the leadership election, and the significant influence he had on both brothers' campaigns. It is little-known that Glasman built the relationships that drove David Miliband's Movement for Change campaign, which saw some 1,000 Labour supporters trained in techniques widely associated with Blue Labour. At the same time, Glasman encouraged his younger brother Ed Miliband to take on the Living Wage – another key policy for Blue Labour proponents – that became the flagship policy for his campaign. In an almost unique position in the Labour party, Glasman remained in contact with senior figures in the rival camps of both Milibands throughout the summer of 2010. Although he was widely assumed to be aiding David's team, he expressed "elation" when his younger brother won. The month after Ed Miliband's victory, Glasman was made a Lord by the new leader, and given the title of "Ed's policy guru" in the press.

After the leadership election the book takes the reader through a series of previously undocumented seminars in the heart of Oxford, revealing how David Miliband didn't just slink away after the election, but remained heavily involved in a significant policy debate. The seminars had a magnetic pull on both brothers and senior figures of Ed's team sat in the same room – a further sign of the growing philosophical overlap between the two brothers. Little-known to many, a significant number of other influential players in the Labour party attended the seminars and became interested in the ideas. The shadow minister for the Olympics Tessa Jowell attended the seminars, as did the former cabinet minister once tipped as leader, James Purnell. The influential Labour MP Jon Cruddas has been closely involved with Blue Labour, and the MPs Hazel Blears and Caroline Flint are also interested, alongside high powered figures in the leader's office such as Stewart Wood. Although few of these characters would label themselves "Blue Labour", many subscribe to its core ideas and have become, inevitably, "tangled up in Blue".

In his interview for this book, Ed Miliband's reaffirmation of these ideas – and his continued personal admiration for Glasman – suggests that this influence is far from over. Blue Labour's relationships with senior staff in the leader's office remain strong. Meetings on key aspects of Blue Labour were being held with Ed Miliband and his team in Westminster over the summer of 2011, and Glasman still contributes his speech writing skills. There is a Sunday afternoon cabinet every few months where Glasman and other "Friends of Ed" discuss party ideas and strategy. Ed Miliband's speeches this year – most notably to the Fabians in January, to Progress in May and Coin Street in June – have clearly articulated Blue Labour themes, with a new and sustained emphasis on responsibility. Similarly his reaction to stories like News Corporation and the phone hacking scandal are influenced by these ideas. One source who works at Labour HQ remarked, "Outside Ed's immediate entourage, there are only two people who have an open door to his office – Tom Watson (MP) and Maurice Glasman."

Of course Blue Labour has its critics too. High profile critics from all sides of the party including Tony Blair, Peter Mandelson, Diane Abbott, Roy Hattersley and Helen Goodman have all spoken out against it. The brand has been portrayed – amongst other things – as xenophobic, sexist, right wing, economically liberal, authoritarian and nostalgic. Undoubtedly there will be valid criticisms to be made of Blue Labour and its agenda, but too many public criticisms have been based on a poor understanding of the ideas themselves. Part of this problem has been down to a naivety of presentation by Blue Labour players, but part of it has also been down to laziness on the part of the media and Glasman's critics. This is a shame, because there is a worthwhile debate to be had about Blue Labour and its ideas. At a time when critics are accusing Labour of suffering from an intellectual vacuum, it offers a contribution about issues that matter to people but are rarely approached by the modern left. However young, Blue Labour has struck a chord. It's worth asking why.

This book aims to tell the real, untold story behind Blue Labour. For all its energy and impact, very few people outside of Westminster know what Blue Labour means, what power it has and what it might mean for the Labour party. This is an attempt to give an honest, impartial account of its agenda and influence so that more people can hold it accountable and contribute to the debate. It does not set out to provide a definition of Blue Labour or offer more than an introductory guide to its principles. The ideas are still young, and it is up to Glasman and the players of Blue Labour to define their ideas in depth. The point is to tell the story of an idea that is still unfolding. The brand's proponents are unconventional, eccentric and refreshingly uncontrolled. The narrative behind these characters, the tensions between them and their influence, is worth exploring. For a political philosophy that puts relationships and place at the centre of its philosophy, it seems strange not to have an account of its own history and narrative. On a very basic level then, it is simply a good story. But it is also a narrative based on a significant and distinctive political theory. It is worth taking a few pages to discuss these ideas now.

The forgotten tradition

Blue Labour starts with a reminder. Although it is a radical new brand, it is grounded in the Labour tradition. But the interpretation of Labour history it offers is not conventional or well understood. For Glasman, a definitive point in this forgotten history is the London Dockers' Strike of 1889. This was at the very dawn of the Labour party, when the organisation was still being formally constituted. Low-skilled workers in the capital were at breaking point over wages that were unstable and rarely left them enough to feed their families. At the end of the 19th Century, bosses wanted to cut crucial "plus" payments for timely work in order to attract more business. The docking companies were hugely powerful and normal channels of petition by individuals were ignored. It was only through coming together as a collective that the dockers were able to fight back. An unusual alliance between Irish and local workers – facilitated by local Catholic and Methodist faith groups – helped broker a strike. The organisers met in the local Labour Representation Committees that became important spaces in the early Labour party. It was a powerful and brave move at a time when the London Docks were an important maritime centre. The British Empire was incredibly powerful at the time, making the security and order of the docks a strategic necessity with truly global significance. Appeals against police were less credible then, and the army and navy could easily have been called in to break the strike. It was a stroke of genius to bring along a Salvation Army band to make the use of force seem unjustifiable and win sympathy and support from the wider public. Against the odds the dockers won, and Labour elected its first MPs to parliament just a few years later.

This story was a phenomenal moment in British history for Blue Labour proponents, but it is much forgotten. For Glasman and others, there are a number of key features that make it worth retelling with greater weight. For a start, the labour tradition originally developed almost entirely outside of the state. Actions like the Dockers' Strike were about communities autonomously organising for their own goals based on their own experiences. Rights may have been enacted through parliament, but they were often hard won from the outside, and were fundamentally about protecting citizens from government power. The modern Labour party, in contrast, seemed to be obsessed with expanding the state. Second, this tradition of community organising was often a way of combating the power of the free market. The dockers were marching against a force that continues to exist to this day; the erosion of wages under the competitive pressures of capital. Again this seemed to Glasman to be a major contrast to the last Labour government, which he believed had become complicit with the unbridled power of the City. Third, the labour movement was led by a more diverse range of social groups than it is today. The dockers were working people, often operating in conjunction with a diverse range of groups from civil society, including faith leaders and charities. For Glasman, New Labour's rule was elitist, technocratic and managerial. Blue Labour believes the party would do well by remembering where it came from, in support of the historian GDH Cole's interpretation of the Dockers' Strike:

> what the British workers wanted was not a purely political movement conducting its propaganda in Marxist phraseology to which they attached no meaning, but rather a movement which would directly express their industrial grievances and aspirations in language and in demands which they could readily understand.

Blue Labour believes that the roots of this tradition extend back well before the foundation of the party to the early 19th Century and before. Indeed, in Glasman's contribution to *The Labour Tradition* ebook in 2011, he argues that Labour's values and traditions go back as far as Ancient Greece. The Aristotelian emphasis on virtue, democratic debate and the moral value of vocation and citizenship are essential axioms of the labour movement. Rightly or wrongly, Glasman traces these traditions through the Tudor-commonwealth statecraft tradition of the 16th Century, which he said was "self consciously Aristotelian". Here too we saw a "politics of practice" as communities spent time balancing interests within the realm, developing apprenticeships and organising to slow the enclosures. Glasman also saw the Balliol Commonwealthmen of the early 20th century – the likes of GDH Cole, RH Tawney and Guild Socialism – as part of that narrative. Alongside this, Glasman added a second strand of Labour "ancestry": the English tradition of liberty. Defined as the period after the Norman Conquest, Blue Labour remains fiercely proud of what Glasman calls the Ancient Constitution and the "Rights of the Freeborn Englishman".

Glasman believes that this tradition offers a powerful basis for Labour renewal:

> always begin with the tradition, that's the orientation of Blue Labour. Whenever I develop anything I will always read from within the history of the movement and try to locate the argument within the traditions, that's a very MacIntyre thing, so I am a nutter for the Labour tradition as the best political tradition that we have because it's paradoxical, it's plural based, it's committed to liberty and democracy and those tensions within it have been mediated democratically by the party at it's best… and I argue that Labour was always, it was founded as an organised party of working people, so the community organising tradition I'm looking at as a really distinctive part of the Labour tradition that we lost.

But not all of Labour's past is appreciated in equal measure. In the most controversial move of Blue Labour's interpretation of history, Glasman believes that the party's proud tradition began to go off-course in 1945. For most party members, the founding of the welfare state and the NHS after the Second World War was one of the party's greatest achievements. For Glasman, the post-war settlement was – in some senses – the beginning of the end:

> there was a wrong turn in philosophy, a wrong turn that affected Labour which was the move to idealisation and abstraction that was all about law and process.

This is not to say that Blue Labour is against the NHS or indeed an important role for the state. What it is against is the way that these measures were introduced, and the new top-down system of managerialism that accompanied these systems. Yes the NHS was unconditional, unquestioned and free at the point of use. But in Blue Labour's view this approach was damaging, not just because it was liable to abuse, but because it failed to empower the recipients concerned. By receiving help through the actions of a benign but wholly anonymous state, individuals were denied a sense of ownership over their own improvement, and the self-esteem that would accompany it. It seemed inconsistent with a movement that had always relied on participation, contribution and self-organisation. Yes people had to make an indirect economic contribution to the state services they now received, but they were not required to make any behavioural change. According to proponents of Blue Labour, the new nationalised industries also failed to empower workers through representation. Although Blue Labour is criticised for embracing what some believe to be a right-wing critique of the NHS, this point about the new nationalised industries was made regularly by the Trotskyist left in the 1970s.

This analysis represents a significant challenge to the Fabian Left and journalists like Polly Toynbee. The welfare state was too hierarchical and controlling in its approach, and this, Glasman thought, was reflected in Labour's language. The values of liberty, equality and later numbers and targets didn't resonate with the public. They were not visceral, and there was no emotional connection. Words like honour, duty and friendship disappeared from public discourse. Individuals were not citizens to be empowered, but consumers to be served. Although Ed Miliband is always careful to premise his remarks on Blue Labour with a defence of the state, he does genuinely believe there is something to this point. The party, he argues, needs to find a more meaningful way of talking to people:

> Love I used a lot in the leadership campaign, love and compassion and I think those words are important and friendship and solidarity which I think is another important word… often I talk about responsibility. It's not about responsibility to the state, I think that's the most important thing, the responsibility is to each other, other people in your community, you know, so when someone rips people off in the banks it's actually about letting down your responsibility to other people, other citizens, I think all those concepts are important, very important.

Then there was a second wrong turn in Labour's history. According to Blue Labour thinkers, the modern Labour party became enthralled with the power of the market. Under their analysis, this betrayal was just as great as the party's new-found obsession with public spending. Unlike the creation of the welfare state in 1945, it was less easy to locate an exact date when the Labour party became, under Glasman's analysis, "enthralled with the City". Working as an academic at London Metropolitan University on the edge of Liverpool Street, Glasman personally witnessed the uncontrolled power of the Corporation of London, the deregulation of the banks and the domination of financial services under Labour's time in power. But the real culmination of this complicit relationship for Glasman came in the banking crisis of 2008 and 2009. When Gordon Brown bailed out the banks, Glasman was horrified. The party that emerged by organising against the destructive powers of capital had now handed over billions of pounds of public money to the City. This didn't just seem unjust or inefficient. For Glasman and Blue Labour thinkers, it was treachery against a tradition. Later, Ed Miliband would show sympathy with this criticism. Stating that Labour was "too reticent about criticising the market" when it was in power, the party leader believes that Blue Labour might offer a solution:

> it's about bringing people together and creating that sense of belonging and sometimes globalisation, there are big forces out there that people don't control you know, undermine that sense of belonging, part of the role of government is to help people in the face of that very big change, not to say you know you kind of "stop the world I want to get off" but actually say, those forces need to be shaped.

Glasman clearly saw himself as a guardian of these traditions, which he believed were under threat. A final tradition worth mentioning – less well documented than the others – is the Catholic Social Tradition. The decline of this tradition was highlighted in 2009 in an influential speech by the Christian theologian John Milbank called – significantly for *The Labour Tradition*'s ebook – the "Politics of Paradox". Milbank's lecture lamented the decline of the Catholic influence in the country, arguing that its collective, community-based philosophy could be an important force in resisting unfettered globalisation. Instead, he argued this tradition had been usurped by a Protestant focus on individualism. What was needed to shake up the status quo, Milbank argued, was a metaphorical "Dark Knight" along the lines of the Batman figure in Christopher Nolan's film – a "genuinely noble outlaw-guardian who must pursue virtue in uncorrupted secrecy". This image would prove to be a striking parallel to Glasman's later position in the Lords. Milbank argued that the dark knight might need to maintain a deliberately "outlaw" status that would allow him to say the unsayable without feeling the need to "appease the masses". As someone who saw himself as a guardian of faith traditions and community organising against capital, Glasman would clearly take inspiration from this metaphor.

The Blue Labour agenda

Through the Labour tradition, Blue Labour asserts that there is a chance of building something better. Although its philosophy and its policies are yet to be thoroughly documented by its leaders, a consistent narrative is emerging. From extensive discussions with Blue Labour thinkers, this new philosophy appears to have three pillars.

Pillar One: interests, institutions and identities

Blue Labour starts with the politics of interests. Under the last Labour government, politicians became obsessed with the pursuit of "utility". An economic term, individuals are judged to be seeking the maximisation of their own happiness, most often defined by the number of goods they can consume. Blue Labour challenges that model by looking at individuals as citizens rather than consumers, and addressing their interests rather than their utility. In marked contrast to liberalism, "interests" are not synonymous with what an individual wants, but those components that are thought necessary for a "good life". This is an Aristotelian idea. Aristotle believed that for human beings to be fulfilled or satisfied as citizens, they need to be engaged in meaningful activity that gives them autonomy over their own lives. In another marked contrast to textbook economics, Blue Labour also believes institutions can have interests, which also have a moral component. Blue Labour thinker Luke Bretherton from King's College writes, for example, that a university can have an interest in pursuing the "common good" of education and the virtues associated with it. Educational institutions should be more than a collection of individual students and managers maximising financial gains.

Blue Labour celebrates interests, and their contestation. The biggest threat to society, Blue Labour argues, is the dominance of homogenous, monopolistic interests. The two biggest manifestations of this dominance come from the market and, in certain contexts, from the state. Although capitalism is often pitted as the definitive opposite of state control, for Glasman, they have this important, dangerous feature in common. Both are powerful dominant interests, and they threaten pluralism. It is Blue Labour's contention that the peaceful contestation of interests is not just useful, but essential, for a good society. As Bretherton puts it, Blue Labour is "committing to democratic politics understood as the negotiation of a common life among diverse and often competing interests." This clash of positions is important both for understanding and establishing the "common good" and for giving individuals a genuine chance to engage as citizens.

Exclusion from the debate, under this approach, is a sin. Blue Labour believes in bringing all interests to the table, even those we might find unsavoury such as the far-right English Defence League (EDL). This contrasted massively with the last Labour government's approach. They wanted to eradicate conflict by satisfying as many preferences as possible; Blue Labour wants to embrace them. Any force that threatens to dominate, overwhelm or exclude these interests – whether it comes from the market or the state – must be resisted.

From a Blue Labour perspective, interests are closely connected with identities. This is another affront to Liberalism, in particular to the benchmark liberal philosopher John Rawls who famously developed the idea of "justice as fairness". Rawls argued that to discover the just way to order any society, it was necessary for individuals to throw off their cultural and social attachments and design society impartially under a "veil of ignorance". The reason for this, Rawlsian Liberals argue, is simple. Because human beings are fundamentally equal, there is no space for the tribalism that comes with identity politics – we should not treat each other differently because we come from a certain race, country or culture. This idea has become strongly entrenched in the modern Left. So when Labour MP and Blue Labour friend Jon Cruddas said that his party needed to get back to "faith, family and flag" – an agitational reference to a concept propounded by the right-wing US politician Sarah Palin – many in the Labour party became critical. Although Glasman never used this phrase personally, Blue Labour does have something to say about each of these values, alongside another – familiarity. The recognition of these emotional attachments is where the small "c" conservatism in Blue

Labour comes from, which in turn gives theory its name. However, it is worth noting that Blue Labour does not advocate simplistic versions of these values, and often interprets them in unconventional ways.

Let us begin with "Flag". Blue Labour believes in patriotism. Glasman believes it represents the "ultimate national form of a common good". This emotional attachment to England is not understood in terms of race, but in terms of the country's history, its values and its civic institutions. Blue Labour's patriotism is not based on a blind reactionary feeling or a distaste for the "other"; it is grounded in a love of one's own. It believes that people owe a reverence to the civic community, land and cultural environment that provided the conditions for their own development. As Bretherton puts it:

> I did not create the language, values and legal system or the environmental, economic and political context on which I depend and so I owe the people and place which made it possible a duty of care and respect.

But this is an argument for general patriotism; Blue Labour has a culturally specific attachment to England. Certainly Glasman as well as Cruddas have a real sense of Englishness and the English nation. Glasman studied English history extensively under the tuition of Oxford University's Christopher Hill, focussing in detail on the 16th and 17th Centuries as discussed above.

Blue Labour's appreciation of nationhood is connected to a broader emotional attachment to place. Blue Labour celebrates the territorial commitments communities might have to their local high streets, street markets or supermarkets. Glasman was personally involved in the campaign to save Spitalfields fruit and vegetable market in London, and took Ed Miliband to visit Billingsgate Fish Market in the capital when it came under threat. Blue Labour thinkers talk a lot about the land, the rivers and the coasts. When the Conservative Prime Minister David Cameron wanted to privatise the forests, Glasman was incensed. Blue Labour pits the love and attachment to these places against the forces of the market that seek to "commodify" public spaces by reducing them to assets with a price. It is interesting, however, that this commitment to the local environment does not extend to a preoccupation with climate change, which Blue Labour tends to dismiss as an abstract, global attachment.

Blue Labour also has a controversial attachment to faith. The left might be uncomfortable talking about religion, but Glasman openly says that Jesus was the "most important person" in the labour movement. This is not to say that Blue Labour believes that the state should cease to be secular. Nor does it advocate one religion over another. Glasman himself is a practising Jew, but Blue Labour is fiercely pluralist. During Glasman's time at Citizens UK, an alliance of campaigning civil society groups, he worked with faith leaders of all types – imams and priests as well as rabbis – to help organise congregations for goals they had in common with atheists and agnostics. Glasman said that through this work he came to see faith as an "important moral resource" to be worked with rather than discarded. Faith groups were the only ones who "actually showed up", for example, when it came to campaigning for the living wage. So Jesus is important to Glasman not so much because he is believed to be the son of God, but because he "gave hope to poor people that their lives wouldn't be dominated either by the state or the market". In terms of theory, this was consistent with one of Glasman's favourite thinkers – the Hungarian intellectual Karl Polanyi, who argued that an alliance between faith and labour could help resist the "commodification" of society. Blue Labour argues that working with faith groups in this way is also firmly consistent with the labour tradition.

Glasman then sees faith as a "vital" interest that Labour must "rediscover" to reinvigorate the Labour movement. But religion isn't just crucial in the formation of alliances that help with community campaigning, it is also essential in generating a policy agenda that can bring people with you in a diverse society. The anti-usury campaign, designed to cap interest rates which Glasman helped run with Citizens UK in the wake of the financial crisis, for example, was inspired by the traditions of the Islamic communities that he worked with. A liberal might want to bracket faith when discussing what a community aims to achieve together, but Blue Labour says these identities have something to offer in that discussion. Indeed, Glasman believes that including faith is an essential part of forming a new political agenda to unify a complex, multicultural society. He openly says he wants to "bring a whole range of women Muslim leaders into Labour". Even after leaving community organising to become a lord, Glasman is clear that building these alliances is essential for the Blue Labour project:

each day I have met a Muslim leader from the community

to discuss how a common good politics can be generated where there isn't one and that is a hard conversation but I think that Islam has a lot to say in relation to the political economy, debt, wages, so put the emphasis away from you know the issue of women and the issue of segregation and towards a common good where the Muslim tradition of justice, economic justice, which is very pronounced, can actually have a really strong effect on Blue Labour and then on Labour so that there could be a genuine engagement with the Muslim communities in the country with the mainstream politics and the issue we're getting to is vocational training, how can Mosques and Muslim community partner vocational training with churches.

Another key interest for Blue Labour is family. The importance of such relationships have long been trumpeted by Conservatives, but Blue Labour thinkers are frustrated that this debate has been shut out of their party. This is not to say that Labour's policies have been against the family – it is rather that these policies were expressed as helping families in a functional, economic way rather than celebrating the value they offered in terms of relationships and emotional connection. As Jon Cruddas MP puts it:

why does Labour not talk about the things that give people meaning in their lives, their primary concerns like their family, like the people who they spend a lot of time with and the deeper things that people think about ethically, the sense of honour and integrity and ethics, duty, honour you know?

As with patriotism and faith, there is an anxiety on the

left about approaching this issue. Part of this objection is liberal; the family is the private sphere and the state has no business promoting one model of personal relations over another. The left's concern is also partly feminist. Women have been concerned that when politicians say they believe in the family, they really believe that women should stay at home. But Blue Labour fully supports women's right to work and the case for gay marriage. At the same time, it argues that families foster the most precious and important relationships in our society, and that society suffers if they break down. It does not believe that these two positions are inconsistent. It also says that as important building blocks of society, the family should be the legitimate subject of policy. In particular, families need protecting from the forces of the market. The living wage is held up as a classic example of a "family friendly" Blue Labour policy. Parents should be paid more so that they can spend more time with their children and nurture the relationships that are important. At its heart Blue Labour argues that relationships and family are more important than money, aspiration and career. If any parent – woman or man – wants to give up work to look after the family, this should be an option. Maternity leave is important, but paternity leave is equally so. Blue Labour advocates do not think the last Labour government went far enough in this regard, even with celebrated programmes like Sure Start. The programme has become a means of supporting families in work by giving them free childcare. But Blue Labour thinks it was a poor trade off. Two parents were now forced to go out and work on wages that were too low to make ends meet. It did not promote better family relationships, it just allowed carers to spend more time serving the market.

The final conservative value associated with Blue Labour that has been overlooked is a commitment to "familiarity", understood here as a form of emotional and material stability. Blue Labour criticises the modern Labour party for being obsessed with "progress". Blair and Brown seemed to have a blind faith in evolution; that change was necessarily about the world getting better and "moving forward". From 1997 the Labour government launched huge reform programmes in public services – it introduced tuition fees, academies, foundation hospitals and private finance initiatives to name but a few. Blue Labour argues that some features of our society are worth preserving, and raises the possibility that change can do more harm than good. Perhaps the most striking example of this is globalisation. Increased flexibility across borders has brought huge benefits to urban, liberal middle classes – often the demographic of those in government – who have the skills and finances to access increased travel and employment opportunities. But for those who are less educated or less financially well off, it has often meant an erosion of jobs, wages and autonomy. This analysis is, somewhat surprisingly, shared by former cabinet minister and current chair of IPPR James Purnell. Purnell was strongly associated with New Labour and its agenda of change and aspiration, but as a close friend of Blue Labour, he acknowledges its weaknesses:

> New Labour is quite change manic, the more change the better, what Maurice says is actually of course change is some-times very good and is sometimes going to happen anyway, but the speed at which change happens and the way in which

it happens can be incredibly destructive and therefore you have to think about how you manage change and one of the things that the state, society have done in the past when properly deployed has been to manage change in a way that reduces the suffering that it inflicted and that was something that was almost without the vocabulary of New Labour.

Pillar Two: reciprocity, relationships and responsibility

Glasman says if Blue Labour could be reduced to a sentence, it would be "relationships are transformative". For Glasman, relationships are essential in protecting interests against the emergence of the potentially homogenous, dominating influence of the market and the state. In answering any social problem then, Blue Labour wants to ask *What are the relationships that need to be formed to solve this issue, and how can they be formed?* This is anathema to much Labour party thinking, which usually defines a task that needs to be achieved, and then expects the relationships to follow. This pillar of Blue Labour philosophy is heavily influenced by the American writer and community organiser Saul Alinsky, who argued in his book *Rules for Radicals* that relationships precede action. Indeed with his rather scruffy appearance and agitational approach to politics, friends of Glasman later said that the academic modelled himself on the American activist. In an interview with Ed Miliband in the summer of 2011, the Labour leader actually quoted Alinsky, and paid tribute to his contribution to Blue Labour. Clearly, Ed Miliband believes that such ideas are valuable:

I think Blue Labour is directing us towards values and institutions and things that we didn't talk about enough when we were in government... it's sort of directing us to institutions, relationships, things which aren't just about the values of the market, or the sort of direction of the state.

Blue Labour believes that the founding principle of any relationship has to be reciprocity. Its subscribers have a hatred of unilateral action. One of Blue Labour's biggest criticisms of the modern Labour party is that it allowed the state to give without asking for anything other than an indirect economic contribution in return. For Blue Labour, this wasn't just bad from the perspective of free riding, it was actively damaging to the recipients involved. As Glasman puts it:

welfare state, social state, security protection state, I'm not happy with any of them, so I'm playing with the idea of relational solidarity or the concept that... really animates me, relational reciprocity, that anything that does things for people without asking anything of them is humiliating, so to get a conceptualisation of redistribution, I want strong redistribution that facilitates people doing things with their lives. Now, when it comes and this is I guess you can accuse me of being a bit biblical, when it comes to the widow, the orphan, people with disabilities, I think we should always be there, that's not the point, that's basic solidarity and compassion, but when it comes to the health service we... can't be uncritical with it, the model that we had in 1945 of universal state based, did lead to massive erosion of solidarity, so we have to renew the solidarity for welfare through relational reciprocity. So the critique of 1945 is not a critique of welfare it's a critique of managerialism and how to imagine the renewal of the welfare state where people take responsibility and have more power.

One important example of how such policies might work in practice is the job guarantee advocated by Purnell in the summer of 2011. Currently chairing the left of centre think tank IPPR, the former cabinet minister said he discussed the proposal in detail with Glasman. The idea is to guarantee work for anyone who has been unemployed for twelve months. But if individuals don't take it, then their benefits are cut off. It's important to note that the policy still uses the state – the job guarantee itself is expected to cost some £2.5 billion a year – but it demands a behavioural change on behalf of the recipient. Glasman openly declares himself in favour of such "relational conditionality". For some on the left conditionality is associated with pandering to a populist agenda, but for Blue Labour thinkers like Duncan Weldon, it is a concern that must be addressed:

> it's [benefit fraud] not a huge problem in the British economy, it's not a huge issue for the Labour party, but it is an issue that bothers people, you are getting up every day going to work and know people who aren't doing that who really are in a position who could be doing that and that is a problem and it's something that really does resonate with a lot of working people in the way it doesn't with people in the Crouch End Labour party.

Blue Labour does not attack benefits because they waste huge amounts of public money or because it has a perception

of a "feckless" working class. Blue Labour doesn't like benefits because they leave people isolated without relationships,
which by Glasman's standards is a kind of poverty. Wherever
possible, Blue Labour believes that the state should look to
help people and cure social ills by fostering relationships in
communities. So for example, rather than opening more Sure
Start centres, Glasman would like to see the state facilitating
introductions between neighbours who take it in turns to
look after each others' children. Combined with the living
wage, Glasman believes this would be a better solution than
individuals struggling alone or relying on a state sponsored
centre. Perhaps more controversially, Glasman says the same
is true with families facing disabilities:

> how you deal with you know issues relating to things like
> Aspergers, autism, no effort is put into building up local soli-
> darity groups between parents, no issue in putting an organiser
> in who can organise the parents to develop their own agenda,
> the resources needed, how we conceptualise what solidarity is,
> is purely through the delivery of services, well what we have to
> do is underpin the growth of the relationships.

Although Blue Labour is not against state action per se, it
is massively in favour of communities organising and fighting
their own battles when they can. This belief was heavily
influenced by Glasman's personal experience of community
organising with Citizens UK in East London. An alliance of
fee-paying institutions – including a variety of faith groups,
universities and others – this organisation brings people
together to campaign for change on the basis of shared
struggles and experiences. Citizens UK was widely credited

for the campaign for the living wage – a premium on the minimum wage – being widely adopted across London. This organisation came with its own distinct philosophy, heavily influenced by the work of Alinsky. Glasman said this was the "missing dimension" in his work:

> I got interested in Alinsky, I got, there was this missing dimension to my thought, leadership development, local political action, local democratic organisation, it's missing from this, so I had the general commodification theory but the theory of local resistance was missing and in many ways community organising was hugely important in developing that.

This "relational" approach to politics contrasted massively with the modern Labour party. This was not just in terms of state policy; it was also in terms of basic organisation. Labour's grassroots structures – its Constituency Labour Parties (CLPs) and branches – were often more focussed on bureaucracy and procedure than about forming meaningful relationships that could help organise for genuine change. According to Blue Labour thinker Marc Stears, the Labour party has some lessons to learn from organisations like Citizens UK:

> The Labour party at its best does things for people across the country all of the time it does things for people when it is opposition and when it is in government, if it's in opposition purely and only looking to the next general election it won't be able to serve communities across the country, it won't be able to save libraries, it won't be able to help local communities build new community facilities and that would be

a real shame, I had a fantastic conversation at lunch today with someone from Ed's office and we were saying that what Labour has the opportunity to do what it's done always at its best which is constantly be there to help people when they need that assistance and it should do that in opposition as well as government and it can only do that if it is actually a vibrant community organised movement.

It is a central tenet of Blue Labour that if the party wants to renew for the better it will have to become more relational, but to do that will require a cultural change that starts in the heart of local parties. The work must start in opposition. It is here, Blue Labour says, that experiments will start and leaders will be developed to spearhead change on a national stage.

Pillar Three: virtue, vocation and value

The starting position of Blue Labour is that capitalism is a reality that must be dealt with. It believes that without democratic organisation on behalf of the people, capitalism can lead to a dangerous concentration of power that can undermine people's livelihoods. But it also believes in the market as an autonomous source of value outside of the state. It believes in private sector growth and argues that the modern Labour party failed to do enough to support entrepreneurship and small businesses. For Blue Labour, economic production offers more than wealth creation. It raises the possibility – in the right context – of a kind of moral fulfilment. Careers should be more than a transaction of time for money. There is virtue in work.

Blue Labour presents a damning critique of New Labour's political economy. The entire model, Weldon argues, was built on an unsustainable credit bubble that was overly reliant on financial services and "disproportionately concentrated in the South East". Public investment increased and made improvements, but the money for that investment relied on taxing financial activity that was at best unbalanced and at worst unsound. House prices soared, share prices increased and banks brought in huge amounts to public coffers. This income was taxed and used to fund a massive expansion of public sector jobs. It helped cure unemployment in the short run, but it was ultimately unsustainable. When Lehman Brothers collapsed in September 2008, the bubble popped. The blood supply to New Labour's political economy was cut off.

Blue Labour believes that a fundamentally different political economy is needed. One model that Blue Labour proponents believe we can learn from is Germany. Here is a country where the costs of labour have risen, but a diversity of jobs have remained. Germany has managed to keep a greater emphasis on the productive economy, achieved more balanced growth across the regions and is less dependent on the financial sector. There are three key features of the German model that Blue Labour often quotes. The first is the country's regional banking system. By forcing banks to operate in certain geographical regions, Germany secures capital for local people and prevents it being sucked up and out to areas that already have high growth rates. The second important concept is worker representation on boards. Under the influence of Blue Labour, Ed Miliband is already considering placing workers on the remuneration committees of banks. The idea is that by giving workers a stake in the management of a business, they become more committed to the organisation and simultaneously prevent bosses taking irresponsible decisions. The final lesson that Blue Labour wants to take from Germany is the emphasis on vocational rather than general skills training. Former Labour leader Tony Blair pushed for all skills to be transferable to give people the highest chance of getting a job. Blue Labour says that it is better to give people specialist training so that they receive higher wages. Apprenticeships are an important part of that.

All of these initiatives are open to criticism. It is a basic principle of economics that restricting flexibility reduces productivity. If capital or skills are tied to particular areas or sectors rather than being made transferable, opportunities for improvement are restricted. Finance might get a higher return if it is allowed to move to another region where rates of return are higher; an individual might have more job opportunities if they can move elsewhere – Blue Labour deliberately restricts that. It argues that the quality of work and a commitment to place and relationships are more important than the chance of a higher financial return. If anything is lost in productivity, it is made back in meaning. The more difficult question is whether the German model can remain an option under globalisation. Even Weldon acknowledges that the German Social Market model is in decline. Germany continues to suffer from significant levels of unemployment, and has been criticised for dividing people too early into vocational and academic professions. There is also a question about how replicable it is in the UK when the country – unlike Germany – exists outside of the Eurozone.

Blue Labour also reminds the party that it has a tradition of political economy at a community level. This tradition stretches back far further than nationalisation. Blue Labour believes in community land trusts, co-operatives and worker representation schemes. It also wants to see a return to Labour's tradition of mutualisation. Believing that people should have a stake in the services that they run, one common Blue Labour phrase is "a mutual space not a neutral space". Under this philosophy, participation is as important as outcome. Equity is more important than equality. The state has a role in transferring power, but the people have a duty to take on those assets and make them work for themselves. The state should not be a producer of services, but a distributor of assets. In this way, Blue Labour argues, the state can produce power rather than dependency. So you wouldn't give a single mum housing benefit, but you might give her a stake in a community housing trust.

One idea that Blue Labour is particularly interested in is the "third" model. A multi-stakeholder approach, this model would see all public institutions governed under a tri-partite board. One third of representation would be made up of funders, which could be state representatives or private providers. Another third would be made up of workers who are employed in delivering the services, and a final third would be made up of users. So in a school for example, there would be a balance of interests between funders, teachers and parents. In health services there would be a balance of interests from funders, patients and professionals. The key aspect for Blue Labour is that no one single interest dominates. It differs from the Conservative model of neutralisation, Glasman argues, because it is not a blanket transfer of power to professionals or users. Blue Labour wants to see every interest represented.

Blue Labour and the deficit

Blue Labour has been criticised by the left as a cover for cuts. Certainly Blue Labour advocates do not think that more state spending is the answer to the country's problems, and would like to see a long-term reduction in the deficit. In fact Glasman argues that one of the "biggest obstacles" facing the regeneration of the Labour party is "the idea that the only problem with the last government is they didn't spend enough money" and has spoken out publicly against Keynesianism. Instead Blue Labour wants to see a rebalancing of the economy, and a higher level of private sector growth. Consistent with the second pillar of Blue Labour, Glasman would also like to see people taking more responsibility for their welfare, building relationships in communities to support their own services rather than relying solely on the state. In a further demonstration of his conservative streak, Glasman is open about his visceral hatred of public sector managers, which he believes is shared by the British people:

> I really have a loathing, which I should share with the readers, of highly paid public sector managers they are arrogant, their contempt for the workforce, the contempt for the people that they treat, they supposedly serve, I would like to see much

stronger engagement of people with their services and the shaping of them, I would like to see them as a form of common good, I'd like it to be that when there are riots they don't smash up the Job Centre the local services… it's like a vote from the people who were using the services on what they hated most and they just smashed them, it's brutal and horrible. We have to recognise that to rebuild a civic culture in the lives of the people is vital, so what I'd like to see is Labour not judging itself by how much it has spent, but on the engagement of people in it.

That said, Glasman does not believe in cutting the country's spending overnight. He believes that the policies Blue Labour is looking to introduce – public sector growth and greater community responsibility – will take time to bed down. In the short term then, he stands with Ed Miliband's stance on the deficit:

I don't believe in shock therapy in relation to the deficit, I think what we have is something like shock therapy, there are massive issues relating to the community, so childcare is a massive concern of mine, if you have children whose parents don't care for them, how are you going to get anyone to pay to look after them, so what we do have is state dependant charities but there is no way out of that unless society is drastically rebuilt which is not going to happen in the next 2–3–4 years, so what I want to see and I will get to the point is a commitment to a much more relational welfare system, a great deal more responsibility in it, I would like to see people having a greater ownership of it and taking more responsibility for it and recognising that these things have costs, so I'm roughly as we stand pretty much in line with Labour party policy on this that we are cutting too hard too fast, but not because cutting is intrinsically wrong, it's not an ideological point, it's that we're in such a terrible state that by cutting we ruin the networks that exist.

Filling the void

These then are the founding pillars of Blue Labour's philosophy. Blue Labour rallies against the domination of single interests understood as the commodification of the market and the monopoly of the state. It moves away from the idea that the market takes all, the state provides all and the community makes no contribution. In its place, Blue Labour calls for autonomy and self-determination. It believes that human beings have interests understood as an emotional attachment to place, identity and the moral worth of work and family. These interests can and should be asserted to help produce a politics of the common good. Blue Labour believes that building such relationships doesn't just help deliver these ends, it is also constitutive of them.

Such a philosophy has major advantages to the new Labour leadership. For a start, it offers something new. Labour lost power in May 2010 and New Labour's political economy was seriously brought into question by the financial crisis and the sad reality that, despite huge increases in public spending, millions remained in poverty. Labour was desperate for new ideas, but seemed to be suffering from something of an intellectual blank. Ed Miliband hadn't assume he'd win and was lacking an obvious, pre-prepared policy agenda. Blue Labour could help fill a vacuum. Second – and perhaps more importantly – these new ideas did not seem to rely on extra state funding. At a time when public money was tight and Labour had been labelled as profligately overspending, this was essential. Again, "Red Ed" was anxious to lose his Brownite label, and Glasman's model offered a way of achieving that. Finally, Blue Labour provided a response to the Conservative party's agenda. By engaging in a discourse about community, this was the only set of ideas that parked Labour tanks on the Big Society lawn. Better yet, it was working from inside the Labour tradition, so it felt genuine. Fully formed or not, Blue Labour's philosophy was ripe for the picking.

For more information, resources and to comment visit
tangledupinblue.co.uk

Chapter One

A Pledge to a Mother

Maurice Glasman had started chain-smoking again. He had reverted to sleeping at strange hours, and he was finding it difficult to eat. Late in January 2009, he was spending another sleepless night talking to his wife, Catherine, in their flat in North London. Piles of cardboard boxes filled their living room floor from top to bottom, overflowing with an odd mix of nostalgic relics saturated with memories. The large dark eyes of Jewish relatives stared out from black and white photos next to clothes and old records. A projector and a cinecam sat squashed on top of old oak cupboards; a collection of coats lined with sheepskin hung on the back of worn leather chairs. The room's rusty orange walls and creaking floorboards were barely visible from objects cluttering the room, littering the present with the past. An old toy car without windows – one of the last traces of his dad's bankrupt toy factory – sat silently on the living room shelf. The room smelt of dust and tobacco shavings. Glasman had an incessant need to fidget and smoke. It was late. His mum had kept everything, and now she was gone. She had died four weeks ago. Now Glasman was standing in the middle of the material and emotional fall-out.

It would be wrong to describe Glasman's home as broken or poverty stricken. Stoke Newington Church Street, in Hackney, is renowned for its fashionably independent and quirky shops. Glasman lived above one such funky store with a fluorescent front. Up the stairs in this trendy location, his flat spanned two floors, leading out on to a tiny balcony covered with jasmine and multicoloured plastic clothes pegs where he could sit and talk. His home was not damp or dangerous; it was warm, friendly and well stocked. An old piano and a computer sat in the living room. The yellow walls of his kitchen were inviting; the room smelt of home-cooked food. Half-used boxes of clingfilm stuck out at all angles from well-stocked drawers. Bottles of vinegars and oils filled wooden shelves stretching to the ceiling. Piles of art materials and half finished drawings lay in one corner, a donkey made out in crayons stuck haphazardly on one side. A sign for kosher milk hung on the wall.

But life wasn't easy. Glasman and his wife were struggling to pay off their mortgage and bring up their children. Glasman was working as a professor at London Metropolitan University, a former polytechnic that offered a safe but small salary. When his children were growing up, he would sometimes work part-time to help with the childcare. He'd left his post in a more prestigious university in Italy after his father had unexpectedly died in 1995, and he'd fallen into the first job he could. Catherine was working in TV production, exhausted from the long hours and sleepless nights from her husband's insomnia. He had met Catherine when they were both in relationships soon after his father died. He had inherited a son from her first marriage and she became pregnant within a year. Now Glasman had four children. All four of them – aged between five and nineteen – slept squashed together in one room. The flat was more than overcrowded. A family of six in a two bedroom flat with one toilet, they used to ask the boys to pee in the bath to stop the queue building up in the mornings. For the last two years Glasman had been working hard with Catherine to support his family whilst caring full time for his dying mother who was suffering from a degenerative illness. Glasman said the experience gave him a deep-seated hatred of New Labour's obsession with the "progressive". He was deeply attached to family, and had been let down by change.

Tonight Glasman wasn't just worked up about the loss of his mum. In his first public venture for a long time, he had just come back from a meeting where he had spoken passionately about the banking crisis. Lehman Brothers had folded just four months before, precipitating the near collapse of the global economy. The Labour government had stepped in to bail out the banks, and Brown was already claiming credit for preventing global economic meltdown. But for Glasman, Brown's response represented a disaster of epic proportions. In his eyes, Labour's failure to regulate capital had allowed an irresponsible financial sector to enrich itself at the country's expense, and when the horrible gamble collapsed Labour was giving away billions of pounds of public money to pick up the tab. Worse, Brown was making this regressive transfer without political question or sufficient economic condition.

In Glasman's mind the two events – his mother's death and the banking crisis itself – were nightmarishly connected. Rivie Glasman was a working-class Jewish woman who left school at thirteen. Passionately dedicated to her family and particularly her youngest son, she brought him up to care about faith, tradition and the Labour party. She loyally and passionately believed it was a party for the good of working people. Now, in Glasman's eyes, that same party had made a regressive transfer of wealth at the expense of people like her. In raging against the economic and political crisis, he was simultaneously mourning his mother's death. Her love for the party meant that Labour's bailout wasn't just a scandal for the country; it was also a betrayal of his mother's memory. In a trait that would come to characterise Blue Labour, Glasman would fuse the personal and the political to generate action and motivate change.

Alongside the financial crisis, three other political factors – often global in context – pushed the emergence of Blue Labour at the time of his mother's death. The first was the ascendency of the Conservatives and the emergence of "Red Toryism". David Cameron's response to the financial crisis seemed to be politically effective. The Tory leader was managing to advocate massive cuts without falling victim to an unpopular Thatcherite label. By positioning himself on the side of the "Big Society" rather than the state, Cameron was managing to detoxify the Tory image whilst advocating cuts. One man who had been influential in shaping this agenda was Phillip Blond, the head of the Conservative think tank ResPublica. Blond had championed the emergence of Red Toryism, a new philosophy which advocated a society-based response to the banking crisis. With his talk of mutuals, co-operatives and social conservatism, Glasman believed Blond was colonising heritage that belonged to Labour. Indeed the name "Blue Labour" was in part a visceral reaction to the Red Tory brand. Glasman wanted to reclaim a tradition that contemporary Labour leaders – who Glasman already believed were too focused on the state – hadn't done a thing to protect. Labour was, in Glasman's mind, politically and economically bankrupt. Now the tradition that might help rejuvenate them was being stolen by their opponents. In four months Britons were expected to go to the polls in a general election, and Labour were almost certainly going to lose. His mother had lost her life; now her party looked set to lose power in a defeat that seemed unjustly preventable.

Across the Atlantic, something better seemed possible. Barack Obama's election to the White House was the second important factor in the emergence of Blue Labour. He had made history as the first black president of the US, and he had won through a campaign that had defied the odds and taken the world by storm. Obama had previously worked as a community organiser in Chicago, and now parties across the world were looking at this tradition, how its principles might affect modern campaigning and whether they might be able to replicate his model. This was familiar territory for Glasman. He had long been involved in Citizens UK, an organisation that bills itself as the hub of community organising in the UK. Importantly, it relied on many of the same principles that had influenced Obama. Next to the energy and enthusiasm of Obama's campaign and Glasman's positive experiences with organising in London, Brown's Labour party looked clunking, authoritarian and defeated. The party's organisation was in desperate need of change.

The final reason for Blue Labour's emergence was the contemporary Labour party's inability to provide an adequate response to these challenges. New Labour's political economy was broken, but Brown was simply bent on picking up the pieces. Meanwhile the Conservatives were in ascendency, seemingly benefiting from a selective interpretation of the best of the Labour tradition. Obama might have swept the world on the other side of the Atlantic by building on the community work that Glasman was associated with, but Labour just wasn't getting it. If it wasn't for his mother's personal connection with the party, Glasman might have given up on Labour. But his mother had brought him up with a staunch belief in its values, and in some strange way he felt he owed it to her to turn it around. There must be some way of distancing himself from what the party had become whilst honouring his mother and the traditions of the movement that he loved. Blue Labour would become his way of finding the answer.

The banking crisis

When the City imploded, Glasman was working on its doorstep. He was working as a lecturer at London Metropolitan University, a former polytechnic, teaching some of the poorest and most diverse students in London on the fringes of the capital's financial heart in Aldgate East. Glasman had a longstanding hatred of Labour's intimate relationship with what he saw as the large and unaccountable power of the City, but he was still aghast at the government's decision to bail out the banks in response to Lehman Brothers' collapse. The country was left with a phenomenal debt that would take generations to pay off, and Glasman was outraged that the banks wouldn't be forced to make any significant change:

> in my calculation it was the biggest transfer of wealth from the poor to the rich since the Norman Conquest, it was huge, it was a trillion pounds and there was no negotiation, there was no need to change corporate governance, there was no investment in the country, there was just a direct transfer of cash. So that made me doubly aware of how powerful finance and the banks were in the governance of the British economy.

But what was worse, according to Glasman, was that Brown didn't seem to get it. For Glasman, the collapse marked a fundamental turning point with New Labour's relationship with finance. But for Brown the priority seemed to be about little more than protecting the status quo. By agreeing a multibillion pound bailout, the prime minister proudly – and perhaps fairly – declared that he had averted a potential crisis, the scale of which threatened to be on a par with 1929. Quick to recognise the need for a global response, Brown had helped lead other countries in producing a co-ordinated international response. When the general election came around, the prime minister repeatedly stated that he was the one to prevent financial meltdown. If he hadn't stepped in, his narrative ran, then cash machines would literally have stopped dispensing cash. Safe to say this response infuriated Glasman:

> I remember Gordon Brown saying about it on television that it was the destiny of the Labour party to save the banking system and I remember thinking there has to be a distinction between destiny and fate, roughly, maybe our fate does it,

but our destiny was something else, and just the silence that greeted that.

For Glasman, the bailout represented something deeper and more rotten with Labour's political economy. He had long been suspicious of what he regarded as Labour's complicit attitude towards the City and the power of finance, capital and the banks. Ten years before the banking crisis, he had been actively involved in campaigning against the governance structure of the capital – the Corporation of the City of London – which he felt had become enthralled with the power of finance. Founded as a commune in 1189, the Corporation predated parliament, giving it a huge amount of autonomy over millions of pounds worth of assets. Glasman had witnessed what he saw as the invisible power of the banks taking over democracy first hand when his close friend – the chaplain at London Metropolitan University William Taylor – failed to prevent the Corporation closing down Spitalfields fruit market and turning it into more profitable office space. As far as he was concerned this power made a mockery of London's more formal democratic institutions. Glasman would frequently compare the unaccountable power of the Corporation with the Greater London Assembly (GLA), the formal body elected by Londoners alongside the mayor:

London has the structure of a shanty town, there is one elected mayor and 12 representatives to represent 8 million people, meanwhile the City of London which represents money has a Lord Mayor, 120 representatives, got its own parliament, the guildhall, the Mayor lives in a mansion house, it's the inheritor of the ancient liberties and it's completely at the service of capital.

Glasman had long lost faith in the Labour party as a means to combat the City. In 2001, Labour passed the City of London Reform Bill, a private members bill that was supposed to make the Corporation of London more accountable by introducing a series of measures including changing its voting system. Glasman strongly objected to the legislation on the grounds that it didn't go far enough. Indeed he argued that the new system privileged larger companies by allowing one representative per five workers. In his mind it was a "slavery franchise", and entirely unconstitutional. Alongside Taylor, he got together a petition calling for the clause to be scrapped, and demanding that the City of London fundamentally reformed. Glasman failed, and the bill passed with a 300 majority under a Labour government. Glasman later said that this experience made him realise how "deeply complicit Blair and Brown were with capital".

According to Glasman's analysis, Labour's deference to finance was the cornerstone of a political economy that was having a destructive affect on the rest of the country. During Labour's three terms of office since 1997, the party had presided over a huge expansion of the City. It now had come to dominate the national economy, and made up an unprecedented proportion of GDP growth. The economy had grown more homogenous, with the majority of the country's wealth being concentrated in one small area of the South East. The rest of the country was expected to move or live off the wealth generated in London that was redistributed by the state. Traditional working-class communities in the North and the Midlands had been gentrified with public money redistributed from the South, but they hadn't been fundamentally redeveloped. Manufacturing jobs hadn't been replaced and industrial centres in the North hadn't been regenerated. Where new jobs were created, they were largely reliant on public sector funding. In areas like Castle Morpeth, Durham and Wansbeck, some 50% of working people were now reliant on state employment. For Glasman, the financial crisis didn't just represent a crisis for 2009, it represented the need for a radically different political economy.

Red Toryism and the Conservative ascendency

In February 2009 Phillip Blond, head of the Conservative think tank ResPublica, wrote an article in the cultural magazine *Prospect*, that had limited but significant repercussions. Written in response to the ongoing financial crisis, Blond suggested that the crash was more than an ordinary recession. Rather, he argued, it represented a fundamental disintegration of the idea of the market state that left the political consensus of the last 30 years obsolete. Although all parties would have to adapt to this realisation, Blond argued that the crash had left New Labour "intellectually dead". All Gordon Brown promised was "an indebted return to a now defunct status quo". He might have been Conservative, but he expressed many of the frustrations that Glasman himself had raised about the Labour party in office.

Many of the solutions Blond proposed also overlapped with Glasman's thinking. In his article – later expanded into an influential book – Blond argued that David Cameron should pursue a Red Tory communitarianism. This movement, he said, should keep the party's socially conservative values but embrace a stronger scepticism of neoliberal economics. It rallied against the concentration of power in the market as well as the domination of the state. Social enterprises, charities and civil society should fill the void left in their place. The country should abandon any obsession with equality, and instead give people equity. The aim was not to redistribute, but to give people a stake in society. Business should not be abandoned, but it should be made to work for smaller players. In practical terms, Blond was arguing for many of the policies that Glasman himself would support: relocalising the banking system, helping the less powerful gain new assets and breaking up big business monopolies. He supported the continuation of a nationalised post office. He called on Cameron and the Conservative party to embrace what he called the "Tory tradition", but acknowledged that he was drawing heavily on Labour's history for inspiration.

Once again, Glasman was outraged. For a start, Blond was using the tradition that as a historian and Labour member he had always associated with his party and the labour movement. In the mouth of Blond and later Cameron, the words stuck and sounded void. Second, Blond's theory took the rhetoric but missed the point; Red Toryism did not have any credible means of constraining markets. But what really incensed Glasman was not Blond, but those in his own party. Whilst these precious values and ideas were misappropriated, Labour members didn't seem to be speaking up in defence of their traditions. As Glasman put it:

I really began to think this is the kind of collective madness that we have got and a historical amnesia, these are our historical treasures and we're just allowing our opponents to steal them, enclose them and we were so state-ist that we didn't have anything to say.

While Labour did little to defend its heritage, Cameron ran with it. Glasman watched defenceless as Red Tory quickly became part of the Conservative's electoral agenda under the "Big Society" brand. Although Cameron had other influences – most notably Iain Duncan Smith's think tank, the Centre for Social Justice – Red Tory ideas seemed to be taking root. In November 2009, David Cameron marked these ideas out as his territory in his Hugo Young speech. In this public talk, Cameron astutely acknowledged the benefits the state had brought in the past, but said it had now grown too big, and was crowding out civil society. He acknowledged that Labour also had a rich civic tradition, but that this had "lost out" to a state obsessed Fabianism which came to see government as the answer to all of society's problems. Quoting Blond directly, he made many of the criticisms that Glasman shared about Brown's government, and referenced many of Glasman's cherished virtues as the answer. The "Big Society" was obviously going to be a key pillar in his election campaign, and much of the rhetoric he was using spoke straight to Glasman and his ideals:

When the welfare state was created, there was an ethos, a culture to our country – of self-improvement, of mutuality, of responsibility. You could see it in the collective culture of respect for work, parenting and aspiration. You could see it in the vibrant panoply of civic organisations that meant communities looked out for one another; the co-operatives, the friendly societies, the building societies, the guilds.

unions?
churches?

But as the state continued to expand, it took away from people more and more things that they should and could be doing for themselves, their families and their neighbours. Human kindness, generosity and imagination are steadily being squeezed out by the work of the state. The result is that today, the character of our society – and indeed the character of some people themselves, as actors in society, is changing.

At the time Cameron was also partly acting for crude electoral reasons. His pre-election party conference speech was widely criticised as being reactionary and overly hostile twoards the state. The Hugo Young lecture was an attempt to re-connect once more with non-Tory newspapers in particular. Nonetheless the views expressed were to some extent working their way into the Conservatives' policy making and were strongly espoused by Cameron's most senior adviser, Steve Hilton.

Glasman's frustration came to a head in a seminar with Blond in Westminster's Portcullis House in the spring of 2009. Blond had been brought in to discuss his ideas with a set of left and Labour party activists, MPs and journalists. Glasman was clearly irritated by Blond's presentation, but he was even more annoyed by the reaction of Labour party members in the room. Once again, no one seemed to be challenging Blond's "corrupted" replica of Labour's ideas. Instead, the audience seemed to be disowning their traditions by criticising Blond's work on the grounds that it marginalised the state. As Glasman explains:

He [Blond] was talking and I couldn't believe what I was hearing as a response, he was talking about friendship, solidarity, belonging and all the people on the left were talking about equality, diversity, basically the state, and not talking about the quality of relationships or most importantly, capitalism. No one on the left was talking about capitalism, which you will find out if this goes ahead is a genuinely a life long obsession, so be aware that capitalism plays a central role in the story, and I remember sitting there and thinking sorry I got the wrong end of the stick, I think I remember saying I thought the Labour party was the party where people came together to resist the domination of the rich, I didn't think it was some kind of welfare agency, you know, democratic welfare agency.

Glasman's controversial outburst earned him three friends that day. Although they had known each other before, Glasman's comments marked him out as someone with a politically significant set of ideas. The first was Jon Cruddas, the Labour MP for the seat now known as Dagenham and Rainham, who had stood for deputy leadership, who emailed Glasman after the session. Clearly he was interested in Glasman's ideas, and asked him to come and meet for coffee. Cruddas was not a minister, but he had a distinct following in the Labour party, particularly from the centre left organisation Compass. Interestingly he also had a close relationship with former cabinet member James Purnell and David Miliband. This small network would prove to be very influential in the leadership election. The two developed a strong and meaningful friendship that would develop from there. The second was the *Guardian*'s political correspondent,

Allegra Stratton, who would also introduce Glasman to a number of significant players in both parties. Without her influence, it is unlikely Blue Labour would have risen as quickly as it did, or generated such a strong media profile.

The third friendship was the least likely. In one of the most unconventional but little-known friendships in political circles, Glasman ending up befriending the Red Tory himself, Phillip Blond. Although Blond had his own much grander apartment in North London, he took to coming around to Glasman's crowded flat in Stoke Newington. In a sign of genuine trust, Blond joined Glasman and his family on Friday nights. This was an intimate space where the family lit candles and ate together in honour of the Jewish tradition and rested after a hard working week. Several years later, Blond still refers to Glasman with genuine admiration, calling him a "deeply good man" and a "dear friend". He used to call him up – only half jokingly – and ask Glasman to join the Red Tory camp. This uncanny ability to form unexpectedly warm alliances in unexpected places was to become quite a trait for Glasman.

There was an important political energy in this friendship; the two could make more noise together than apart. The two worked together in tension, going head to head in a public debate billed as Red Tory vs Blue Labour at Conway Hall, and publishing an email exchange in *Prospect* magazine. Later Blond went even further and said that he deliberately helped promote Glasman – whose name was at that time virtually unknown in Westminster – by participating in these joint debates. Blond had always had huge confidence in the significance of his ideas, which he believed would extend well beyond the Conservative party. There were good strategic reasons then, for supporting Glasman and his Blue Labour project. A "sister movement" would help push what Blond saw as a new political consensus:

> I would only win and my ideas would only succeed if there was a similar movement on the left because we needed to create a new centre ground and that takes both sides to agree. Maurice and I genuinely differ which is right and proper and we differ most on markets, so it's not like we agree but I think his insights are in authentic parallel to mine on the left and I know history and I know that to create a new centre ground you need two sides to agree.

Of course there were significant differences in their ideology. Most notably, Blond thought that Glasman was too confrontational in style and too Marxist in substance. He believed Blue Labour lacked an appeal to a British sense of aspiration, and was unlikely to play well with the electorate as a result. Glasman for his part believed that Blond did not take the power of capital seriously enough. He also argued that Blond's model for mutualisation was not sufficiently trans-formative because it didn't include a range of interests. For Glasman, it was important to foster and encourage a diverse number of interests within any organisation. Handing over control of services to workers simply replaced a monopoly of the state with a monopoly of employees. Glasman's model of mutualisation, in contrast, would encourage representation from different groups to encourage pluralism.

It's also interesting to compare the two men's positions within their own parties. On a surface level, they were oper-ating in a similar space. Both thought that their respective parties should change, but both lacked an official position of influence in their chosen institutions to achieve it. But although they were both party political insurgents, it would be a mistake to think of their positions as identical. Although Blond always had more resources than Glasman, he remained a much more isolated figure within his own party. He had none of the significant and close relationships with the leadership that Glasman went on to have. Glasman could see that, for all the bluster, Blond's project was a much lonelier one than his own. Talking to Glasman, it seems as if his affection for the Red Tory was tinted with a desire to look after him:

> [Blond has a] very generous, gentle disposition to him and by far the best way of having a relationship with him was to embed him, for him to come over, he never has a cooked meal, he only has takeaways, was to come over have a Friday night meal, with children, it turns out he is brilliant with children, he gives them quizzes, he and Isaac, can you imagine have a kind of equality of ego, with a five year old child Phillip, he and Isaac can go completely head to head it's brilliant and he's very loving with children.

Obama and community organising

On November 4th 2008, world history was made when the USA elected their first African-American president. Barack Obama's victory shook the world. Defeating his Republican rival John McCain with a majority of some ten million votes, his victory stood out not just because of his race – nor even just because of his initial status as the underdog at the beginning of the contest – but because of the nature and strength of his campaign. Obama's election team pushed the boundaries of new technology, fully embracing the deeper more widespread access to the web. Social media was used to mobilise activists up and down the country in a truly transformational way. Using online tools to facilitate offline action, the Democrats' campaign brought together a ground-swell of thousands of volunteers, gave them the tools to get involved and raised some $650m in a breathtaking number of small scale donations.

For Labour members watching Obama's victory in the UK, it seemed a distant victory. Although the ideologies of US parties do not map neatly on to those in the UK, the Labour party had generally considered Obama's Democratic Party to be their sister organisation. Leaving aside Blair's alliance with the former Republican president George Bush, it was generally believed to be a productive international alliance when Labour was in power in the UK and the Democrats were in power in the US. Despite this affinity, the contrast between the two parties' popularity, morale and organisa-tional capacity couldn't have been more stark. Labour was coming to the end of three terms in office and seemed tired and defensive. Brown had never been chosen by the people in an election; he had simply inherited the throne from Blair. In complete contrast to the oppositional fire of the Democrats, the incumbent Labour party lacked energy, dynamism and popular support.

After 2008 a number of up and coming Labour activists started looking across the water to see if anything could be learned from Obama's campaign. The general election was already on the horizon for 2010, and Labour was in desperate need of reinvigoration. In early 2009 Nick Anstead, a political lecturer at East Anglia, joined forces with the rising Labour star Will Straw, son of then justice secretary Jack Straw, to edit a publication for the Fabian Society called *The Change We Need*. This pamphlet called on the Labour party to copy Obama by removing barriers to participation in campaigning, enabling channels for dissent and giving supporters the tools and information they needed to self-organise. Taken together, the authors argued that these lessons could mark a significant shift in the Labour party that would bring them more in line with the United States model. In its present state, wrote the editors, the Labour party was unlikely to follow Obama's blazing trail:

> Labour's winning formula over the last decade of centralised command and control is at odds with the defining character-istics of the 21st Century. Society is more fragmented, atom-ized and diverse than ever before, yet individuals – particularly the young – use the networks of Facebook and MySpace to replicate the community spirit of old. Much of what Obama achieved was only possible because of the openness with which he ran his campaign and the decentralization of key tasks to his myriad of supporters. Such an approach is alien to the modern Labour party.

Citizens UK

After the American election, community organising and grassroots campaigning were massively in fashion. Stalinistic models were out; open networks were in. The stage was set for change, but very few knew how to achieve it, or indeed how it would work in practise. There was a growing consensus within the party that the organisation needed to evolve, but there was an uneasiness about how this might be achieved.

There was one UK organisation that was well placed to capitalise on Obama's victory. Citizens UK – formerly known as London Citizens – describes itself as the "hub of community organising in the UK". An alliance of fee-paying institutions, Citizens UK members include churches, mosques, unions and universities. These members sign up with the aim of building power in communities to bring about change. Significantly, Citizens UK was founded on similar principles to the Gamaliel Foundation, the Chicago based organisation where Barack Obama himself trained as an organiser. Citizens UK was also seeing a rise in profile thanks to the success of their campaigning efforts across London. Their flagship campaign to promote the Living Wage – a premium on the legally required minimum wage that takes into account the cost of living – was hugely successful and adopted by the city's first Labour mayor Ken Livingstone, and his Conservative successor Boris Johnson. Crucially, Citizens UK was also Glasman's stomping ground.

Citizens UK was an apolitical organisation, but it came with its own very distinct philosophy about the way organising should be done. Like the Gamaliel Foundation, the chief philosopher associated with Citizens UK's approach was Saul Alinsky, and his book *Rules for Radicals* had become something of a bible around the Citizens UK office. It had a distinct understanding of power and success that had been criticised as 'cultish' by less formal community activists, and the organisation's large assemblies – which always attracted a plurality of faith groups – often had a religious feel to them. Citizens UK had a relentless focus on recruiting and developing "leaders", often understood as people who came with a "following" and could maximize turnout at political events. More isolated individuals were considered less useful. It was a results based organisation grounded in power analysis. It was not by any means a charity and had little time for vulnerability. Many of its chief organisers were Oxbridge educated. This model was very different to the model of community campaigning that Obama pursued for his party political election, but that didn't matter. Obama's victory raised the profile of community organising. People were looking for an organisation to explain what it was about, and Citizens UK was more than happy to fill the gap.

Neil Jameson was the director of Citizens UK. Jameson had set up the organisation – first known as the Citizens Organising Foundation – with the aim of reviving community organising in the UK in 1989. He'd previously qualified as a social worker and worked in Wales and the Midlands after taking a degree in politics. Glasman had caught Jameson's eye during his campaign against the City of London in the House of Lords. Years before he would be given a peerage, Glasman was simply rallying from the gallery. Jameson used to come and watch. He told Glasman that he'd never reform the City by lobbying parliament. The only way forward was through organising and building alliances and community relationships. Although Glasman was quite bemused by the attention at first, Jameson clearly made a strong impression on him, and he remembers meeting him well:

> a little man with a beard walked into my life and said you
> know "Hello, I'm Neil Jameson, I represent London citizens"
> and I said I'd never heard of him. He said "Have you heard of
> Alinsky?" I said no. He said "Are you interested in community
> organising?" I said no, I don't know who you are. He said
> "Why don't we meet?" and I was in the mood of "do we have
> to". He said I'd like to, and so, and he came every day and sat
> in the House of Lords and watched this and his point to me
> was you are about to lose and I said I never expected to win,
> and he said "Why are you doing it?" And I said well it's very
> interesting, and someone has to stand up to them. He said I
> agree but why don't you come to a meeting next week, we're
> very interested in developing the idea of a living wage and I
> was, he was quite insistent.

In spite of his initial scepticism, Glasman went along
to a meeting at Citizens UK at the organisation's office in
East London, and quickly found that he was able to gain a
huge amount from it. Here was an example of an institution
that was not just well grounded in civil society, but also won
tangible results for its members. Glasman remembers his first
meeting was a discussion about the living wage:

> I went to this meeting which was overwhelmingly Catholic,
> low church, black majority, Muslims, there was one trade
> unionist there and the concept was on family life, a topic that
> at that time made me come out in a sweat, so I thought I was
> going to walk into something where they were going to tell
> me I really shouldn't enjoy sex or something and I saw these

ordinary people, saying they didn't have time to look after their children, their parents, basically I saw the living wage being formed and that was really again transformational, I said wow, that's very interesting and this began in about 2001 I just started going to Citizens UK meetings and living wage campaigning.

Citizens UK would often bring together community leaders – representatives of member institutions – to hear their concerns and help them organise to fix them. So for example, when the living wage was made a priority, particular businesses and organisations were targeted. Cleaners and faith leaders would ask for a meeting with senior figures to discuss an increase in wages, and if it was refused, they would gather outside their bosses' offices and make their demands more publicly. When a meeting was granted, testimony would be presented, and pledges hopefully won. Glasman spent some ten years with Citizens UK, and during that time he was able to see community organising delivering results. Their methods continued to win the living wage for workers at major institutions including Barclays and HSBC.

Glasman started getting more heavily involved. Citizens UK – originally known as TELCO in reference to East London location and later as London Citizens – was conveniently located around the corner from his university's campus. After teaching he could easily walk by the office and participate in meetings. He also quickly started getting involved in training sessions, taking members and trainees on walks of the City to explain the power of capital. Outside the office, Glasman would also be out networking, trying to engage a wider variety of institutions to join Citizens UK, meeting

Imams, community and faith leaders. Jonathan Cox, a young organiser who joined Citizens UK as a full-time staff member some time later, remembers meeting Glasman in 2008:

> I've never met this guy before and we went into this seminar room at London Met and Maurice was sat there in his usual way, in his scruffy clothes and, you know, popping out every 20 minutes for a fag. He did this really interesting paper on Saul Alinsky and the importance of faith institutions in community organising. He had been on a journey – someone who is Labour through and through, having got a bit disillusioned by the Labour Party, and also someone who had grown up in the Jewish tradition but who was not practising and was rediscovering the importance of faith. He was running the Faith and Citizenship program at London Met. I think London Citizens provided him with a meaningful way in which he could find a way of doing politics while honouring these institutions.

Unlike Cox, Glasman was never a professional organiser. Citizens UK had a very distinct set of criteria for measuring a good leader, and Glasman didn't always fit the bill. But according to Cox he had serious qualities that Citizens UK leaders did recognise, and couldn't ignore:

> we judge a leader by a number of things, and firstly do they have a following? Well he didn't have a following, but to be fair he [Glasman] has worked with the discipline and has tried to cultivate that. Secondly, are they relational? We don't encourage a dictatorial kind of dominant power model of a leader who says: "right you must follow me now" and he's very good at that. The missing link, I guess, was the institution, but

he presented much like many of our best leaders within our institutions – he is always meeting people one to one, building relationships, he doesn't get involved in programs and bureaucratic activity. He focuses on building relationships, and thirdly, he understands power and understands the way we organise and has a passion for it, and has an anger, a cold anger, grief I suppose about well, in his case the power of the City, the dominance of money and commodification and stuff he now talks about. Also he was influential on the London Citizens agenda. He helped us enormously in bringing his expertise and his political mindset to things. But to be fair to him he didn't win all the arguments – there were times when he wanted to push certain things or downplay other things and because he didn't come from a big institution he didn't always get his way and he was gracious about that.

Citizens UK wasn't just an interesting introduction to organising for Glasman. It was also a source of cultural and intellectual enrichment. With its emphasis on relationships, power and action, Glasman later said that the philosophy behind Citizens UK outlined by Alinsky was the "missing link" in a lot of the academic texts he had read. Specifically, it gave him a concept of leadership, training and action, to hang on to the more conceptual and abstract texts that had inspired his politics in the past. One very influential mentor in this process was Arnie Graf. The head of the Industrial Areas Foundation (IAF) in Baltimore, Graf had studied under Alinsky and had an almost mythical presence for Citizens UK, whose living wage campaign had been inspired by his work in the United States. Even after Glasman left Citizens UK to take up a position in the Lords, Graf remained a key mentor to Glasman. This would later help push Alinsky's philosophy into the minds of senior figures in the Labour party. By 2011, Graf would even be invited over to advise the new Labour leader, Ed Miliband.

It was also through organising that Glasman rediscovered his Jewish roots. As part of his attempts to meet community leaders and encourage leaders from all faith traditions to join Citizens UK, he started frequenting synagogues. In a reclamation of his family heritage, he tried to create something of a revival of the radical Jewish tradition that had existed in the East End. This reconnection with his cultural history was, Glasman said, compounded by what he believed to be a "new anti-Semitic left" in the East End. His students were making casually racist remarks, and when the East Ham cemetery was desecrated in 2000, very little was done:

> I went to Jewish Schools and Synagogue, until I was 18 I'd never met anyone who wasn't Jewish as a social equal, either it was superiors, teachers, or we had a lady who came to the house to do cleaning… when I got to university I was desperate not to ever mix with Jews but that was because I'd had enough, so my family thought this was a moment that would pass, but it didn't pass. Then I'd lost the rage and I had lost the sense of being brought up in a ghetto and it was good to reconnect, so I think the huge amount of my, Alinsky is Jewish, Arnie Graf is Jewish, they were all secular Jews, very long tradition of Jewish community, self organisation… I realised I learnt a huge amount of this from my background but you don't wait for other people to found a school, you found a school, you educate your children, you organise your own burial societies, you organise your food, basically this is a community that is

built on self organisation and mutuals. I just never viewed it that way, so it was rediscovery, reconnection with who I was. Then when I realised there was this weird attitude to Jews I was like, Fuck it, I'm a Jew there you go, if you don't like it, the belligerence well if you don't like it you can fuck off really.

But Glasman wasn't just building links with Jewish communities. He formed relationships with a diverse range of faith and non-faith leaders, meeting the heads of mosques and educational establishments as well as synagogues. Glasman was particularly fond of Jameson, Taylor and another organiser called Matthew Bolton. Glasman had always described himself as a bit of an outsider; in Citizens UK Glasman had found a genuine set of new friends. It wasn't always easy to balance his new found love of community organising with his four children – the work was all unpaid and Glasman and his wife Catherine didn't have much money – but they were happy. Later Glasman looked back on that period with affection:

… I found a happiness in this kind of political action, so I really made friends and real public relationships with imams, with Muslim leaders, Christian leaders and we started winning living wage, then Catherine Howarth left and Matthew Bolton took her place and things got even better, and this was a wonderful few years where just we were immersed in those local struggles and how to win them and what you have is this tremendous tactical action and you can imagine I was really drawn to forms of what some people thought was public humiliation of officials but worked well. Then I realised the happiness of seeing local leaders coming on and not being able to speak in public at first and then negotiating with the Mayor and negotiating with, and growing, it was a great period and in many ways this was just you know, we didn't have any money.

When Lehman Brothers folded, Citizens UK quickly realised that they could play a major role in the response. The status quo was shaken; this was the perfect opportunity. Glasman had already had years of experience helping to organise against capital. Citizens UK quickly set up a series of listening exercises with its member institutions to come up with a policy platform. Although Citizens UK demands were supposed to come from the bottom up, Glasman was heavily involved in defining the agenda. As well as extending the organisation's campaign for the living wage and introducing regional banks, a new "anti-usury" campaign called for a 20% cap on the cost of lending, a legal code for lenders, an investment of one per cent of the taxpayer bailout to go to mutual lending and a financial literacy plan for schools. At a time when Labour was struggling to come up with an original response to the financial crisis, Citizens UK was succeeding in generating a new and popular agenda:

> the people's response to the financial crash and that was the result of an enormous spurt of work, living wage plus interest rate cap, plus regional banks and I was really, that was an intense engagement and that is where I began to think to be brutal this is a strategy, this is a, and the Labour party hadn't developed a strategy but this group of, it was interesting the radical political economy was coming from faith groups at the time, I was very interested in that and then I got this research

grant to actually write about it, and that is another story, with Neil Jameson going no, no, the price of writing about it is you have to do it.

Grounded in Citizens UK, these proposals were never destined to be abstract ideas left on a shelf. In November 2009, these demands were put straight to political leaders in front of 2,000 community leaders in the Barbican Centre in Moorgate. All three of the main political parties were there, alongside the British Bankers Association, major employers and London's mayor Boris Johnson. In a victory for Citizens UK, the Conservative shadow treasury minister Greg Hands promised to cap interest rates charged by store cards and to consider restricting lending on other financial products with "egregious rates". Once again, Glasman felt he had achieved a result. It was his first experiment with generating a practical political economy, and it would go on to form many of his ideas for Blue Labour and Labour's 2010 manifesto.

It is difficult to overestimate the influence of Citizens UK in Blue Labour. Community organising – and Alinsky's philosophy – became a significant part of Glasman's theory and ideas. Listening to community organisations had given him a sense of people's priorities in the wake of the financial crisis, and a set of tangible policies that might help. More significantly, Citizens UK had given Glasman a grounding in a new relational form of politics that contrasted with what he saw as Labour's technocratic and managerial status quo. The fact that Citizens UK took off at the same time as Obama's presidential victory meant that other people were ready to listen to it. Community organising was to move from a quirky and little-known technique used in the darkest corners of the inner cities to a mainstream phenomenon that – through Glasman – would capture the attention of senior figures in the Labour party. In particular, it would go on to gain the attention of both Miliband brothers in the leadership election.

The failure of Labour

The post-crash Labour party was in a mess. Despite an initial bounce in the polls for Brown after decisive action in the face of the financial crisis, his leadership was once again being brought into question and his popularity was draining in the polls. In May 2009, the party was hammered in the local elections. In a worrying premonition for the general election, the Conservatives took Staffordshire, Lancashire, Derbyshire and Nottinghamshire from Labour, all of which had been strongholds for the party for over twenty-five years. Senior figures were calling for Brown's resignation, and by the summer of 2009, divisions were beginning to snap. The communities secretary Hazel Blears resigned just before the elections and James Purnell, the high profile work and pensions minister, quickly followed suit, actively criticising Brown's leadership in his resignation. Two former cabinet members – Patricia Hewitt and Geoff Hoon – wanted to remove Brown through a secret ballot, supported by Charles Clarke and others. Two senior backbenchers, Barry Sheerman and Graham Allen, broke cover to demand the prime minister's resignation amidst increasing rumour of full-scale backbench rebellion. At a time when the party desperately needed unity to respond to the financial crisis,

Brown's government was splintered.

The leadership, organisation and morale of Brown's government couldn't have presented a greater contrast to the energy surrounding the Obama campaign across the Atlantic or the engagement of Citizens UK on the streets of London. Obama's campaign and Citizens UK seemed grounded in civil society and open to new and growing alliances; Brown's government was rife with division. Obama's and Citizens UK's campaigns were about action outside of the state and – in the case of the living wage and Glasman's anti-usury work – actively challenging the market. Meanwhile the Labour party was focusing on saving the market and protecting the state. Obama and Citizens UK seemed full of energy and new ideas; Brown's party seemed to be clinging on to a cracked and broken status quo.

Despite all his success at Citizens UK, Glasman felt frustrated by this state of affairs. He was angry because he felt the Labour party should be offering something better. Because of his obsession with the history of the labour movement and his emotional family connection with the party itself, he felt that this was Labour's moment, and he blamed Brown for letting the country down. Although he was not yet in a position to influence whether Brown was ousted as leader, he made it quite clear that he wanted him to go:

> everybody knew that this was a slow motion train crash and nobody was prepared to act, I have to put on public record how intensely disappointed I was with [Peter] Mandelson with that regard who suddenly took the chief position of loyalist knowing completely that what you had was a guy who was two faced who spoke morally to the public and acted

like okay a psychopath in private, but there was a complete disconnect between the words that came out of his mouth, particularly after he refused to go to the country in whatever it was 2007, people then knew that what you had here was the dithering megalomaniac which in political terms is the worst thing you can have, someone who longs for power but can't make a decision.

With Glasman's frustration came a sense of injustice. He fervently believed that the agenda he was collating with Citizens UK was in tune with the Labour tradition, and that it should be adopted more widely. He believed that the policy proposals he had been working on represented a more genuine manifestation of the party's history and values than anything that was going on in Number 10 at the time. Old-school party machinists like Brown were damaging the party by refusing to recognise its roots. Now that tradition was being colonised by Conservatives, and no one in Labour seemed to be speaking up.

The death of a mother

For Glasman all this had been building alongside his mother's illness. The banking crisis had reached fever pitch in conjunction with her degeneration. In some darkly appropriate way, the events felt connected. The fall of the City and Labour's inability to react became associated with the personal decline of this woman who brought up her son to revere the Labour party. Glasman's mother was dying, and as she deteriorated so did Labour's ability to serve traditional working-class supporters like herself. In both cases, Glasman felt he had to be a silent witness, losing both something personal and political in a way he couldn't control. Later Glasman would say his mother's slow decline was a visceral reminder that sometimes it's better if things stay the same:

> if you want to know the root of my hostility to the "progressive" she had an illness called progressive supranuclear palsy which just meant she lost control of, she couldn't speak, she couldn't eat, she couldn't walk and yet her brain was unaffected so I had to witness her silent degradation it was just terrible and that's when my joke first started the last thing you want to hear when you go to the doctors is it's progressive, and this idea that progressive meant that things were going to get better began to irritate me, don't you get it guys, life is difficult and hard and then you die. So that was very terrible.

Glasman would care for his mother for two years. His wife Catherine, who was initially rejected by his family for not being Jewish as well as for her previous marriage, was finally accepted. She helped tirelessly whilst also looking after the children. Glasman had always been the mischievous child in the family, making his mother laugh in spite of her illness, and right to the end Catherine said her husband remained "relentlessly optimistic", talking to her about his campaigns at Citizens UK and the living wage to keep her attention.

It is hard to explain how influential Glasman's mum really was on her son. Fiercely proud of her heritage, she'd steeped him in Jewish tradition. Incredibly family orientated, she had brought him up with huge warmth and affection alongside her four sisters. When describing his childhood, Glasman openly celebrated her working-class roots. With true "tough love", she scolded him and scolded teachers who criticised him even more. She instilled in Glasman a strong sense of education, forcing him to stay on when he wanted to leave school and join a band at fifteen. Importantly, she had also given him a strong sense that, for better or worse, the Labour party was very much his "natural home".

When she finally did die, on 31st December 2009, Glasman said he was knocked out. No matter how much it had been expected, it just felt "as if she would go on forever". After keeping up a relentless optimism for so long, Glasman's energy was sapped. He reverted to childish sleeping patterns, getting up at 5pm in the afternoon. He stopped organising and taking calls. He had no heart for anything apart from smoking and talking to his wife Catherine. They would talk about his sadness at the loss of his mum, and about his anger with Labour. Now his mum was gone, he realised the two were related. He was grieving for a political as well as a personal loss:

> We were having conversations about what am I going to do, how am I going to deal with this grief, why was I so bereft about the politics, everything looked terrible, banking collapse with no significant political move, Conservatives claiming all that was best about Labour's heritage, a completely at the time, which still lingers in my language, managerial, bureaucratic, democratic, elitist, political labour ruling class.
>
> … And so I felt double the grief in relation to what I was going through, I felt the grief from my Mum and the grief of this relationship that never really been with labour.

This then was the context that gave birth to "Blue Labour". At a time when most policy derived from a shrewd analysis of calculated polls, Glasman's ideas couldn't have presented a greater contrast. The context for the emergence of Blue Labour might have been determined by global events, but the actual catalyst for its birth was intensely personal. In Blue Labour, Glasman saw a chance to honour his mother and the traditions she believed in. In committing to change the Labour party, he could fulfill his duty as a son. What was uncanny was that Glasman and Catherine seemed to recognise the momentous nature of the realisation, not just on a personal level for Glasman and his grief, but on the wider political stage. At the time Catherine desceibed it as a "magic key". Blue Labour had never been mentioned in the corridors of Westminster or the press; it was simply a hidden secret between a man and his wife behind the walls of a small overcrowded flat in London. But somehow they knew that it would spread, with significant ramifications for the Labour party and perhaps the country.

Chapter Two

A Speech to Remember

Methodist Central Hall sits calmly amidst the bustling political heat of Westminster. Inside, its giant domed ceiling stretches high overhead, opening up a grand circular space that pulls the audience together. Some two and a half thousand people can fit inside its walls, packed in on royal blue chairs on deep red carpets. The lighting is dramatic. Huge lamps suspended on twenty-foot metal chains hang from the ceiling. Buildings like these were built to accompany words like honour, spirit, valour and veneration. Audiences have looked down from the hall's grand old balconies throughout the pivotal moments of the 20th century: the Suffragettes met here to campaign for women's votes; Gandhi rallied for Indian independence; the inaugural meeting of the United Nations general assembly was convened here in 1946. The weight of history fills the room. The building itself was erected in remembrance of John Wesley, a Methodist minister famous for open-air preaching. On 3rd May 2010, it was the prime minister's turn to enter the room. Gordon Brown was set to take the stage.

It was three days before the British nation was set to vote in the general election. Battered in the polls, exhausted and demoralised, Brown's government was all but broken. Cabinet members had resigned, morale had dropped and the country's debt was being lambasted in the press. With polling day in sight, it was one of the lowest stages of the prime minister's career. But on that day, something snapped. In an explosion of latent energy, Brown gave what became widely reported as one of the best speeches of his career. The man who had been compared to Stalin managed to speak – perhaps in desperation – from the heart.

The formal leadership debates – held for the first time that year – seemed stale in comparison. The media wondered where he'd been hiding this side of himself for so long. Although it was not enough to save Labour from electoral defeat, it rallied the troops like little else in his campaign. The speech got over 165,000 views on YouTube and kept attracting over 10,000 views a week. It was flagged as the top political speech by Google. The energy of this speech was thought partly responsible for Labour's 6% bounce in the polls a week before the election.

Although the speech itself is well remembered, the story behind it is little-known. Brown's lines were originally penned by Glasman. Still fewer know that it was the relationship between Ed Miliband and Glasman that was able to get the speech in front of Brown in the first place. The emotional reckoning on that day was the result of fraught but invisible work behind the scenes. Citizens UK organisers worked for months to make it happen, but three days before the assembly was due to be held, it was nearly called off. Even the minute before Brown went on stage, the prime minister wavered and almost backed out, a vivid sign of how unreliably erratic he had become.

The prime minister's speech did not win him another term, but the ramifications of his words and the relationships behind them would reverberate throughout the Labour party after he left office. Indeed, they continue to colour the Labour party to the present day. In an emotional display none could predict, the assembly would raise the profile of Citizens UK and capture the attention of those at the top of the party. The invisible facilitator of all of this was Maurice Glasman.

Glasman meets Ed Miliband

Glasman first met Ed Miliband in the autumn of 2009, one year on from the crash. Glasman's mother had by now died, and he was busy trying to balance his family with his work as a lecturer and his time at Citizens UK. Meanwhile Ed Miliband was secretary of state for energy and climate change, and was trying to meet his demands as a minister with another task – writing Labour's manifesto for the 2010 election campaign. Ed Miliband had become interested in the living wage campaign organised by Citizens UK, and had agreed to meet Glasman to discuss whether Labour might be able to use it. He was introduced by Patrick Diamond, a mutual friend who was a special adviser for Ed Miliband at the time. Diamond's interest in poverty and policy had led him to Citizens UK, and he and Glasman immediately hit it off. Now Diamond said Glasman and Ed Miliband should meet, and the minister was running late. Glasman was shown into a private room to wait:

> I remember he [Ed Miliband] was 30 minutes late, they put me in a room where all the lights went out, so when they came to get me I was asleep, I'd fallen asleep in a dark room because they had light sensitive technology

Apparently Ed Miliband never found out about this. When the young minister was finally ready to meet, his assistant Simon Allcock came and woke Glasman up with a "very gentle" nudge. It was laughed off as a natural result of the department of energy and climate change trying to save emissions.

Despite the initial hiccup, results suggest it was a successful meeting. In the 2010 manifesto, Ed Miliband and his team went for a number of the policies Glasman had been working on at Citizens UK including interest rate caps and community land trusts as well as the living wage. In another little-known discovery about Glasman's real influence on the Labour party, Diamond said that he came once a month to Downing Street and was "very influential" on the manifesto. If Labour had had a stronger chance of winning, or if the press were more interested in policy rather than Brown's personal unpopularity and manoeuvring behind the scenes, perhaps these policies would have been given greater profile. As Diamond explains:

> his [Glasman's] ideas were certainly influential in the 2010 manifesto, not just the living wage, but in number of different areas: mutualism, tackling credit card debt, expanding credit unions. There were also ideas under discussion about how to reform the banking sector after the financial crisis. There were actually a series of bold and radical measures in the manifesto,

far more than has been appreciated: for example, policies to restrict overzealous mergers and takeovers that destroy value in the corporate sector. Maurice's positions, not only his policy ideas but his vision of a good society, had a bigger influence than has been acknowledged. Everyone thought Cameron would win and it wouldn't really matter, but actually a lot of it was there at the beginning, and can be developed ahead of the next election through the policy review. Ed was enthused by the ideas that Maurice was proposing. Ed and Maurice got on, but the reason Ed wanted to pick up Maurice's ideas was because he saw them as strategically advantageous. They were very useful to the Labour party, and that is why the relationship has worked.

A number of reasons have been put forward to explain why the two were able to connect so well. For a start, Glasman had no idea that he was meeting the future leader of the Labour party. Glasman would later say that it was "beyond his conceivable imagination" that Ed Miliband would stand against David Miliband. Similarly, Ed Miliband had no idea that he was meeting someone who would lead a high profile call for the party to change direction. This ignorance meant that both men were relaxed and free to talk without the burden of expectation or high pressure roles, although the meeting shows that Ed Miliband was already seeking a range of new contacts long before he declared he was standing for leadership.

The second reason for their compatibility was a shared belief in the importance of social movements beyond Westminster. As Sunder Katwala, head of the Fabians puts it, Ed Miliband "gets the community thing". During his time as secretary of state for environment Ed Miliband was running campaigns on climate change and actively calling for activists and voters to form a movement that would help push green issues up the agenda. He appreciated that that pressure from outside government would give his arguments inside more weight.

The final reason is perhaps deeper and more cultural. Ed Miliband and Glasman were both from intellectual Jewish families. Both had close and tumultuous relationships with their relatives and both were younger brothers. Both played the role of the mischievous affectionate ones in families where older siblings struck a more serious tone. Although the nature of their families was very different – Glasman's mother was a practising Jew whilst Ed Miliband's father was fiercely secular; Glasman's mother was staunchly Labour whilst Ed Miliband's father was deeply communist – the two clearly had a shared understanding and heritage. Glasman said they never explicitly talked about Jewish culture, but there was a certain kind of moral compatibility, a shared ethical response that was instinctive enough to feel cultural. As Glasman put it:

> with Ed, he just gets a jolt and he's got a bit, there is a strong moral, response, intuitive response to things which I recognise, but I wouldn't want to over theorise that, that's got many roots including secular socialism… I have no means of judging where that is from but it's certainly something I relate to. He doesn't calculate on that, he just says "I don't like that…[it] just doesn't sit right", he has a restlessness.

More than anything, Ed Miliband was relational. In the

space of that rare less-pressured moment, Glasman remembers quickly moving beyond the business of the living wage, and straying into other subjects that mattered to both sides:

> Yes, so Ed said living wage was what he wanted to talk about, and we spoke about living wage and he gave every indication of getting it, but also we spoke about language, he said you know what's wrong with our language, I remember that and, and suddenly we were speaking about friendship and loyalty, about love, it was a really lovely meeting, it was very sweet, my impression coming out of it was that it was a really sweet meet, you know.

Glasman would later compare this meeting with Ed Miliband with his initial introduction to his older brother, which occurred just a few months later in 2010:

> with David I felt I was dealing with potentially a future leader of the Labour Party, and with Ed, I was dealing with a future friend, you know, someone who got it, who got it with living wage, was very interested in organising, so I had a very careful relationship with David, much more political, but a much more carefree relationship with Ed, who I considered to be you know, just someone who is going to help develop things.

But Glasman's connection with Ed Miliband was set to be built on more than personal sympathy. Glasman quickly gained a deeper respect for Ed Miliband when the cabinet member succeeded in getting the living wage on to the Labour party manifesto. This took Glasman by surprise. Not only had Ed Miliband "got it", he'd also managed to deliver.

As an organiser committed to judging success by results, Glasman was clearly impressed. Later he described it as a "huge and courageous act", believing that behind the scenes Ed Miliband had to battle fierce opposition from Brown and Mandelson. The news was splashed over the front page of the *Daily Mirror* – an emotional as well as a strategic victory for Glasman, given his desire to speak to working people. It was a tangible victory for Labour policy. His personal affection for Ed Miliband that had been clear from the first meeting was strengthened by a sense of shared achievement.

Glasman meets Purnell

Whilst Glasman was forming relationships with Ed Miliband, he was also forming crucial bonds with members of David Miliband's camp. From a distance this move could easily look deliberately calculated, but it wasn't. With no knowledge that the brothers would stand against each other, Glasman's relationships were not the cynical products of strategic foresight. He never pursued a relationship with David Miliband directly. He simply made friends, and made the most of introductions when they were suggested to him. It is true that Glasman loved community organising and wanting to promote Blue Labour where he could, but he would argue he was true to his philosophy. Relationships preceded action, not vice versa.

One man in particular was crucial in forming the link between David Miliband and Glasman, and that was former cabinet minister and current chair of the think tank IPPR, James Purnell. It was an unlikely friendship. In office Purnell had been known as a rather cold and formal minister, staunchly Blairite in his politics and politely credible in what appeared to be a limited, almost managerial view of politics. But in a move that clearly chimed with Glasman's beliefs, he had walked out of cabinet a year before the general election in protest at Brown's leadership. Purnell had been specifically concerned by the party leader's take on the deficit, which he felt was not being addressed with sufficient concern. More widely he was concerned that Brown would lead Labour to a calamitous defeat. Unusually for a public figure, Purnell showed more of an appetite for politics and ideas after he withdrew from an orthodox career. When he met Glasman he had left Westminster politics to take up a post at the think tank Demos where he was researching how to reinvigorate the left.

Purnell and Glasman had slightly more in common in their personal lives. In office, Purnell had been chair of Labour Friends of Israel. Like Glasman, Purnell had been educated at Oxbridge before he started his career in politics as a researcher for Tony Blair in 1989. Glasman and Purnell were both born in London, but had a strong connection with the continent. Glasman had taught in Italy, and Purnell had received most of his early education in France.

Needless to say, when the *Guardian*'s political correspondent Allegra Stratton first suggested to Glasman that he meet James on the back of his debate with Phillip Blond, Glasman himself was sceptical:

I was initially extremely reluctant thinking that he [James Purnell] was a Blairite yuck thing, horrible to children and poor people in his pensions reforms and meeting James was just brilliant, I really liked him. I really enjoyed his company, I really learnt a lot from him and it was a real friendship

But according to Glasman, Purnell was "widely misunderstood" by him and others. It is obvious that Glasman took an awful lot from their friendship in a way that casts fresh light on Purnell as a public figure:

James was one of the very rare things a very real friendship developed, it was brilliant, I was initially quite sceptical and that's a really strong, and very interesting… His honesty, his ethical sense, his mix of compassion and unsentimentality, his experience of government, I've learnt a huge amount from James.

Perhaps even more surprisingly, the feeling was mutual. Purnell instantly warmed to Glasman. The two met at Glasman's conventional haunt, the Bar Italia in Soho, in the early summer of 2009. It was where Glasman asked all his contacts to visit. With a supply of high quality coffee, Bar Italia also had a space for Glasman to sit outside and smoke in the bustling heart of the city. The conversation flowed so easily at the first meeting that the coffee turned into dinner. They went for a meal at Yalla Yalla, a Lebanese restaurant around the corner, and kept on talking. Glasman's ability to discuss history and high theory as well as the daily political grind appealed to Purnell. After that point the two began to meet on a near-weekly basis, discussing ideas. From their first meeting, Glasman was able to find warmth in the former minister known for coldness. A few years later, Purnell's affection for him is still evident:

most people who meet Maurice you don't speak about policy stuff straight away, we spent a lot of time getting to know each other. It felt like the conversation started at 54 miles per hour and then went way beyond 60 very quickly and we didn't agree on lots of stuff, the first or second time we met we had a long conversation about parliament and stuff which I disagreed with him a lot on but it was an interesting disagreement.

This unlikely relationship was to have many consequences, with one particular introduction standing out. Glasman brought Purnell to Citizens UK. In what seems like another counter-intuitive move for a former cabinet minister once spoken of as a future leader, Purnell was not only open to the ideas of community organising, he also agreed to go on one of Citizens UK's training events the same summer he met Glasman. The five-day training Purnell attended included sessions on the understanding and forming of relationships, and their vital place in building and challenging power. Purnell later described it as "amazing". It turned out that he was more "relational" than one might expect, but also that community organising of this kind had a greater grasp of realpolitik than anyone might have thought. The training was about much more than developing a "fluffy" neighbourliness; it was about organising for results. This struck a chord in Purnell, who insisted that he learnt a lot from it:

> lots of people can see the politics in a very PPE kind of way, very "go away and work out the answer and then implement it with the use of papers", well actually what it reminds you of is actually it's as much about power as it is about ideas and about how you build relationships to do that. It made me think if I

had my time again in government I would spend about a third of my time doing, building strong relationships you have to work with. That's one thing you have in opposition, you can have really strong relationships and you work together and then in government you get into lots of different departments and it becomes harder and harder. Once you know someone and trust them you go with them on their journey.

Of course this relationship was very much two-way. If Purnell got something from Glasman, then Glasman certainly benefited from Purnell. A very close friend of David Miliband, Purnell would prove to be – along with the Labour MP Jon Cruddas – the chief source of connection between Glasman and the older Miliband brother. It also raised Glasman's standing within Citizens UK. Through Glasman and his unlikely friendships, Citizens UK knew they had the attention of heavyweights within the country's leading political party. In a remarkable testament to the power of relationships, Glasman had gained significant influence in the most unlikely places, winning affection with key players across the spectrum of the Labour party. In something of a pattern, the rather unconventional academic was propelled straight to the top of the party through little more than meaningful friendships.

Citizens UK

Assemblies had always featured heavily in the work of Citizens UK, but they were unconventional events. In a normal assembly, people are brought together to celebrate or recognise an achievement that has already been achieved outside of the room. In Citizens UK assemblies, the business is done in the room itself. High profile power holders – be they politicians, business leaders or others with influence – are invited to Citizens UK assemblies to publicly commit to the audience's demands. Rather than flattering their guests with deferential treatment, Citizens UK's visitors are placed in the middle of the stage and asked if they will commit to working with the organisation's members and their demands. In such a public position, it is difficult to say no. In exchange, the power holders gain a link with the community and a better reputation. Turning down an invitation would also be a reputational hit.

The demands made in the assembly are a culmination of a much longer process. The member groups of Citizens UK – churches, mosques, unions, universities etc – are asked to hold a series of "listening exercises" in the run up to the event itself. Through one-to-one and group meetings, the idea is to eke out the members' priorities to put to relevant power holders. Past examples of such "asks" include the living wage, caps on interest rates and an end to child detention. These demands must be tangible and pragmatic to help with accountability. The assembly itself is then the culmination or crowning moment of these listening exercises. Although most of the negotiating on the asks takes place behind the scenes, the public commitment makes them difficult to neglect later. It's important to understand their format, because they would recur again and again in the leadership race.

Citizens UK had always had a focus on the capital, but other branches were springing up across the country. In the year of the general election, Citizens UK was pushing some

2000 member institutions. It was clearly an organisation on the rise. It had held its first mayoral accountability assembly in 2008 and another on the financial crisis in 2009. The mayoral assembly had brought together all of London's candidates and managed to get the future mayor, Boris Johnson, to commit to working with them on the living wage and an amnesty for illegal migrants. Approximately six months before the general election, Citizens UK decided that their model for the mayoral London Assembly could be transferred to a national level. The dream was to put the future prime minister on stage and make him pledge to work with the organisation before the general election. They had never attempted anything on such a scale before.

A core group of approximately thirty people were brought together to form a cabinet and drive the assembly forward. They were charged with pulling off what was set to be the biggest political action in their group's history, and it would require massive co-ordination. According to Citizens UK organisers, their first task was to "pack out" a giant hall to prove that they were not just an average community group. Citizens UK's moral leverage over politicians is underpinned by their credibility as an organisation well-rooted in civil society. It was essential that their connections with communities were visible and public in the room, both from within London and the wider UK. Then there were speakers to book, media coverage to co-ordinate and listening campaigns to run. From January 2010, this General Election Assembly cabinet was meeting once a week. Although a core group was present at most meetings, a total pool of some seventy activists would come in and out. They included community leaders as well as Citizens UK staff, here on after known as "organisers". Significantly, one member who was there every week was Glasman. One organiser, Sophie Stephens, said he played a key role:

> Maurice was important and he is a very smart guy. He was able to give us a lot of political context from a Labour point of view. He understands community organising and he had been very much part of our work and the living wage campaign so he could nuance our "asks". He was important, came to every meeting and was a big part of conversations with people like James Purnell. He'd had experience of this work and had a very good political understanding of what was going on. But he was one in a team of organisers and leaders who were organising the Assembly – his was one voice amongst many others within Citizens UK.

Methodist Central Hall was quickly chosen as the venue. Filling the 2,500 capacity hall meant that Citizens UK organisers would have to start taking bookings for seats before the party leaders could confirm their attendance. The chosen date was May 3rd. A bank holiday Monday three days before the election, the date was strategically chosen to help maximise turn-out and receive national press attention. Invites were quickly signed off and sent to party leaders.

January, February and then March quickly slipped away. Cabinet meetings kept being held, tickets were allocated and the member institutions decided on their priority asks. The agenda and the guest list was nearly set. It was decided to ask the party leaders about the living wage, the ending of child detention, an amnesty for illegal migrants, community land trusts and street safety, alongside the normal demands for further meetings once in office. There was only one problem: the leaders weren't confirming. As Stephens recalls:

> We had people ready and the Citizens UK members were excited and committed. Organisers kept totting up the turnout numbers to 2500 and we kept checking who was coming and then asking again – there was a lot of going back and forth with members. But we still hadn't got confirmation that any of the party leaders were coming. Two weeks before we had no confirmations but the team leading the assembly decided it was going to run either way. We did all that we could, the event even included a choir with Muslim, Christian and Jewish singers all coming together, but we knew it was going to be a pretty big flop if no big business was done on stage because none of the politicians turned up. Citizens UK members were coming to do politics.

Citizens UK had written to Brown's office several times, and were repeatedly told that they were "considering it". Cameron and Clegg were waiting to hear from the prime minister. Citizens UK staff were trying to use every connection they could to pressure a promise for attendance. Purnell in particular was brought in here, saying later that he was "emailing and texting constantly". Glasman was also making the case wherever he could. When April arrived, organisers were getting desperate.

Then just a fortnight before the election, Cameron finally bit the bullet. Citizens UK was in touch with Conservative spads (special advisors) in Central Office, particularly Rohan Silva, who seemed genuinely interested in developing links that were more commonly associated with Labour, having recently taken up a position on the traditionally left-leaning think tank Demos. It was obvious that the assembly could be sold as part of the Tories' commitment to the Big Society. The community agenda was taking hold, and this would be a good opportunity to see Cameron rolling up his shirt sleeves and addressing the people. Very quickly after Cameron committed to come, Nick Clegg followed suit. According to Stephens, the organisers were "absolutely overjoyed". Now at last the ball was rolling.

But Brown still wouldn't commit. Several reasons were put forward as to why his office remained wary. For a start it was quite an unconventional ask; the assembly didn't follow the normal format. Brown was highly unpopular at the time and exposing the prime minister to any kind of risk was considered to be a bad idea. As Purnell explains:

> they refused for ages, I think for a number of reasons, one is it was a big ask, it was a bit late in terms of getting into the diary, you know when you are running an election campaign you are running, it was in the last week you know giving a whole day to that was a big thing, they didn't really know what it was going to be like, it was mysterious, it sounded dangerous.

Another reason behind Brown's office's hesitation was the agenda. Specifically, there was a worry about the organisation's asks on immigration. Coming straight from Citizen UK's diverse membership base, one of the public asks – the "sanctuary pledge" – was to end child detention. Another ask, from a campaign known as "Strangers into Citizens", wanted to grant an amnesty for illegal migrants in the UK. Although these issues appealed to Nick Clegg and the Liberal

Democrats, who had planted both these issues firmly in their manifesto, it was a sore spot with Brown, whose Labour government had presided over the incarceration of asylum seekers and had done little to integrate informal migrants. Brown's office must have been worried about coming across as too hard on immigration for the audience in the hall, and too soft on immigration for the public watching his pledges on TV at home.

Behind the scenes, Glasman argued that the focus should be taken off immigration in the assembly to increase the chances of Brown's attendance, but other organisers felt that this was unfair given the work and attitudes of their members. According to lead organiser for the Citizens for Sanctuary campaign, Jonathan Cox, this had nothing to do with Glasman's commitment to ending child detention. It was simply a tactical point about getting results:

> basically I think he [Glasman] thought, probably with good reason, that Brown was less likely to come if the immigration issues were on the agenda because he wouldn't want to be faced with the... issue and, you know, the general narrative of that. That's my assumption, and what Maurice insinuated to me afterwards was that was one of the reasons that it took so long for Brown to confirm that he would attend.

Less than one week before the assembly, Brown still hadn't committed to come. Citizens UK's organisers were worried that with only two political parties represented, they might have lost credibility with the public and their members. But the cracks were opening. With Cameron and Clegg's commitment to attend, the media interest was snowballing, increasing pressure on the prime minister's office to get on board. False rumours started spreading on Twitter that Brown had changed his mind, raising hopes and dashing them again. As well as Purnell and Glasman, many Citizens UK staff were Oxbridge educated and well-networked with links to political advisers and politicians. They all pushed every line they could.

But Brown's office pushed back. One organiser remembers receiving a brutal response stating that receiving the invitation nine times "was not going to make Brown nine times more likely to come".

Bigotgate

Just when it was least needed, "bigotgate" hit the news. On 28th April, Brown was on an election tour in Rochdale. He smiled politely when 66-year-old resident Gillian Duffy voiced her concerns about immigration, but when he got back in his car, Brown described the grandmother as a "bigoted woman" and added that the whole meeting had been a disaster. It was only once he got into a BBC radio car later that day that he realised the microphone he had been wearing for Sky at the time had been left on. His comments were broadcast everywhere, and caused national outrage just over a week before polling day.

For Glasman, it was a mistake that epitomised everything that was wrong with the modern Labour party. The ordinary concerns of working people weren't being addressed; voters were only given a chance to speak when the prime minister was wheeled out as part of the electoral show. When they did get a chance to voice their concerns, they were dismissed as bigots. But it was the two-faced nature of it, with Brown saying one thing to a voter's face and another behind her back, that really did it. The offhand comments tapped into a national feeling repeatedly picked up by the polls that politicians were disconnected and lacked authenticity. They might need the support of the people, but they secretly disliked and distrusted them. They were out of touch.

If getting Brown to the assembly had looked difficult before; it now seemed impossible. Glasman was fuming. Fiercely protective over the party in the wake of his mother's death, he was now witnessing Brown insulting its supporters and refusing to attend an assembly that he felt could turn the party around. As the son of a minister, Glasman believed that Brown should have known better. Out of a sense of sheer frustration, Glasman sat down and started to write:

> it was my job to try and get Brown to come and that was a nightmare, no one would reply to my calls, nothing doing, so we had an assembly, conceivably where we would have London Citizens, David Cameron, and Nick Clegg and no Labour representative, at this stage I was going completely mad, so I just sat down one day and I wrote a speech for Brown in an attempt to say come and do this, and I sent it to Ed.

In a moment of frenzied passion, Glasman wrote all the words he wished Brown would say. It was a speech grounded in the Citizens UK tradition – it was about Brown's personal life, his motivation and his identity. It referenced his childhood and his upbringing. It went right through Brown's campaign as a student to get a decent wage for university cleaners to the introduction of a minimum wage during his time as chancellor. It talked about his role in pressuring authorities to disinvest in apartheid South Africa, and the power of the people. It was emotional, heartfelt and genuine. And it was sent directly from Glasman to Ed Miliband's inbox three days before the assembly was due to take place:

> I wrote a real London Citizen speech, a real testimony speech talking about him who he was, what his values were, if you ever doubt my loyalty to the party you will know I wrote a speech for Gordon Brown. Ed got it to Gordon Brown and he changed it, but he did it, he really did it and it was really something, for me, I realised I'd never written a speech for a politician before, I was blind, it was kind of a talent moment, I can do this.

And by something that felt like a miracle, Brown responded. Less than seventy-two hours before the assembly was due to take place, Neil Jameson, head of Citizens UK, finally got the call to say Brown would be coming. On top of that, he said he would be giving Glasman's speech, although it would be adapted after a backwards and forwards exchange with Kirsty McNeill, a trusted player in Brown's office. Safe to say the redraft came back with a lot more numbers in it, but it was there. Once again, the relationship between Glasman and Ed Miliband had yielded tangible results.

The assembly

The message that Brown was finally coming reverberated around Citizens UK's institutions, generating a final wave of excitement that rippled throughout their members. Citizens UK's members came from a huge range of communities to hear the leaders speak, pulling up on buses and trains into the heart of Westminster. For many it was their first direct interaction with politicians at that level of power. After months of hard work, Citizens UK had succeeded in their plan to pack out the room. Methodist Central Hall was heaving. Jewish groups sat with Congolese groups as people of all faiths and ages sat down together. The seating plan went awry.

When the event kicked off at 3pm, Cameron took the stage and made a strong contribution. Months of negotiation meant that he knew what he was going to be asked, and the organisers knew that he was going to commit to ending child detention. Nick Clegg followed suit. Cameron had been honest with the assembly about not being able to promise an amnesty for illegal migrants, but Clegg declared his commitment to this in full.

As Clegg left the stage, the audience broke into a loud and overwhelming applause. Shouting and cheering, they knew what was coming next. The prime minister had arrived, and he was waiting in the wings. This is what they had been waiting for. Many of the people in the room were from traditional Labour strongholds in deprived communities. The chance to see this man – their man, the prime minister of the UK – was a huge moment. The weight of the election campaign and the personal pressure on the battered leader fused with the emotional heat of the room. The crowd knew that through the flashing cameras and rolling videos in the room, hundreds of thousands of people around the country were watching this speech with them just three days before the nation went to the polls. The energy had reached fever pitch.

But backstage in the dark, Brown didn't see this. Nor did he believe it. According to one organiser, he was rattled. He didn't want to take the stage whilst the audience was still clapping:

> Brown turns to a colleague and says "I'm not going on". My colleague asks what he means. "No, no I'm not going on because they are clapping for the last guy. I'm not going until they stop," Brown replies. I guess it must have been the demoralisation after Duffy and the burns throughout his campaign. The organiser said to him "They are clapping for you – the standing ovation is for you" so he comes back to the stagedoor and he realises it is for him – it's for the Prime Minister of the UK – and he walks through into the hall. The people, filled up to the balconies, start a standing ovation and people rush Brown to shake his hand and take photos.

It must have been one of the more publicly emotional moments in Brown's career. The public that was used to seeing him as hard and obstinate saw a spontaneous warmth as he walked on stage and, unprompted, embraced the child who gave the first testimony about what it was like growing up in a family of cleaners that were simply paid the minimum wage. It was on the back of that testimony that Brown stepped up to do his speech:

> I know that in your work as community organisers you share

testimony with each other, so please allow me to testify today to what I believe, and to tell you who I am. I am the son of a Church of Scotland minister. He taught me my father that life was about more than self interest, that work is about more than self advancement, that service is about more than self service, that happiness is about more than what you earn and own. My parents taught me that the fundamental values of taking responsibility, doing your duty, being honest and looking out for others. That is the right way, it is your way and it is my way.

Glasman said the atmosphere was "electric". In a room teeming with ordinary people, Brown somehow refound his roots and connected with an energy that had been smothered by the pressures of Westminster. He stumbled on one or two of his words, but his emotional fluency was as great as it had ever been. In that moment, the obsession with polls and perceptions was gone. In its place was a personal story about his identity and beliefs. Glasman might not have clicked with Brown, but he was somehow able to articulate the prime minister's story better than he was able to himself. From the passionate shake in his voice, it was obvious that Brown was taking on Glasman's words and pouring himself into them. He was able to trace a path through the history of popular movements, stretching from the abolitionist movement to Citizens UK's struggle for the living wage today. He did this not in an abstract way, but grounded in his own personal experience:

When I was a student the two causes I worked for most were to force my university to disinvest in Apartheid and sell on its shares in South Africa, and I also ran a campaign for decent pay for university cleaners. And across the years I feel like my life has come full circle because when I became chancellor of the exchequer the first thing I was able to do was to create the minimum wage for the first time in 100 years – justice for the low paid. And the fight continues, and that is why we have said in our manifesto that the minimum wage rises at least in line with earnings, it will reach £7 on reasonable assumptions by the end of the parliament. Because we must lead by example Labour is pledged to go even further by asking all Whitehall departments to back the campaign which you have led to which I pay tribute: the campaign for the living wage. And your campaign has shown something even bigger, that a community is more than its buildings, more than its institutions, more than its fabric. A community is thousands of acts of friendship and service and compassion to each other.

Towards the end of his speech, Brown ended with the most personal note "… *You will always find in me a friend, a partner and a brother.*" He publicly committed his party to the living wage and supporting the work of Citizens UK. In a turn around from his original position on immigration, he later made a commitment in writing to end child detention.

And the crowd felt it. They gave him a standing ovation and rapturous applause, cheering from the balconies and the floor. They knew what Brown had been through, and they heard who he was. Some 300 people stayed behind afterwards to pour out their thanks and admiration in the evaluation.

The speech didn't just make waves with the public. Purnell, who had so recently resigned from Brown's government, personally called the prime minister to congratulate him on the speech. But this wasn't the most significant call that was made that night. Whilst Glasman was still on stage in the middle of the assembly, his phone started to ring. Ed Miliband had watched the whole thing broadcast live on BBC parliament. Glasman picked up:

Ed just rang in and said "That was great". Now if I think back I think what I said to him was "Okay you can imagine what a speech like that would sound if it was given by a genuine leader" and I didn't mean that you [him], I was just thinking at that moment, just inhabiting that space, imagine if we had a real candidate, I didn't give a thought to David or Ed as a truth, it took me quite a long time to work out how that had penetrated into a Labour consciousness.

You said you first sent the speech to Ed Miliband?

Yes it was originally to Ed, I think Ed was personally relieved that what he thought was the real Gordon Brown had some public expression, it was whoah, more on the lines of what a great thing to do together, that worked and then it was yes see ya, and I didn't hear anything more for a while, so it took time to seep in but for me it was blimey I can do this.

What about David Miliband?

No comment.

Even before the leadership race started, Glasman had a shared personal connection with Ed Miliband, and little response or interaction from his brother. The dissatisfaction with David Miliband would only grow as Glasman spent more time with him, but it started early on. In fact, Glasman says he was disappointed that David Miliband hadn't moved against Brown earlier in the day:

> I have you know, respect for David, [but] he is one of the people who could have moved against Brown and didn't and that has always come back to bite, you know he didn't seize the moment, not that I talked to him about it but he was an obvious person who could have moved and didn't… it didn't fill my heart with hope and joy.

After the assembly Citizens UK organisers gathered together in the Abbey Orchard pub in Victoria to celebrate. Sitting at the bar overwhelmed, they watched their assembly being played over and over again on the news channels. It was leading all the coverage. The *Guardian* called it "barn stomping". It got 165,000 views on YouTube and exploded on social media. It went up by 10,000 hits a week and Google flagged it as the political speech attracting the most traffic. Most importantly, it produced a 6% swing in the polls just three days before the election. And it came from a man who had never written a speech before.

Speech writing was to prove an important art for Glasman. It was a long way from delivering an academic lecture, but looking back, he said that it was informed by his time at Citizens UK. Whilst academic discourse frustrated him, he was excited by the discussions that happened through organising. He was used to hearing people's stories and telling them. The trick with Brown then was simply to cut the academic voice, and speak from his experience:

the enigma with Brown was I knew where he was from, he was the son of a Church of Scotland minister, it's straight forward, I know the difference between right and wrong, honesty and dishonesty, you don't pass by on the other side, I wrote just big letters, the response I got back initially was "Isn't this a bit simple?" You know? But what I knew was in any effective political speech you have to speak from your own experience and it seemed to me the only experience left for Brown was sitting as a child in his father's church and watching his father speak... then I googled him and found this stuff, you know, he was basically a living wage organiser at university, that he was arguing for proper pay for the cleaners and the cooks and he was an anti apartheid organiser so I just put that in... he has a story to tell, so testimony, what we do in London Citizens, always testimony, it basically, say who you are you have got all the way in this election campaign and you have never told anyone who you are.

After the general election, Glasman did get a chance to see Brown face to face. It was in July 2011, and the former prime minister acknowledged Glasman's work. It would not be true to say that the two men made their peace with each other. Glasman left the meeting feeling that his prejudices of Brown had been confirmed:

I did meet Gordon Brown now I'm not saying the two things are related but I met him and then got flu, I really got it for 2 weeks it was a shocker, basically what he wanted to talk about was the internet, African children, the role of the internet in ending poverty, it was just one of the most dissatisfactory conversations that two people could ever.

Did he thank you for the speech?

Yes, he did say I really appreciate it, it wasn't, there was no issue, it was just the awkwardness, there he was, there I was, I had the whole, my side, and he, it was like being with a deeply depressed person, that was the overwhelming sense that I got but a depressed person who had not yet got the end of the beginning of the depression. So I spoke about face to face organising rather than internet, the conversation didn't get anywhere.

As for McNeill, Glasman wrote to her asking if she'd like to meet. They had produced an incredibly successful speech together – he thought it might be the start of a productive friendship. Glasman said he never got a response:

it was such a battle to get him [Gordon Brown] in there the scars from that lingered and then you know I was waiting to be asked to write the next speech but that never happened so they then went on to do two completely unmemorable speeches. Since then for my sins I've never missed an opportunity to identify Brown as the problem and I think there is you know dislike and I'm sorry for that but I think they can't recover unless it analyses the problems with Brown.

This silent spurn had very little consequence for Glasman. His influence was set to grow regardless. Beneath the media spotlight, the events of that night reverberated throughout the Labour party. Citizens UK, little more than a dot on the political map for a couple of Labour players, had now exploded onto the Westminster stage. It was the organisation of the speech that unlocked Brown's leadership, and the Citizens UK office was deluged with enquiries from all parties. Stakeholders from all sides were intrigued about the organisation that generated a different type of leaders debate. Within Labour circles, a ripple of questions went through the ranks: who was this organisation? Where did this speech come from? For many significant party members, this was the first time they had ever heard of Glasman.

Most significantly, the assembly captured the attention of the two key future candidates for the leadership. This would have ramifications for the nature of the Labour party itself and the role of community organising in the party. For Ed Miliband, it was another example of his partnership with Glasman achieving tangible results. Together they had pulled the Labour party back in the right direction and given the party a crucial last minute boost in the polls. For Glasman, it didn't matter that there were other factors influencing Brown's change of heart – the media pressure, Purnell, the combined efforts of Citizen UK lobbyists – in his mind, Brown's momentous acceptance to come to his assembly and give his speech was somehow connected with his relation-ship with Ed Miliband. Together, it was possible to challenge the Labour party. For David Miliband, it was an eyebrow raiser. Citizens UK was already on his radar thanks to James Purnell, but after May 3rd the organisation went from the latest hobby of a former colleague to a force that was capable of gripping national attention. At the end of that assembly, both the Milibands felt that this organisation had something to offer. Almost at the same moment David Miliband and Ed Miliband saw Glasman as a potentially powerful ally as they prepared to fight for the leadership of the Labour party.

Chapter Three

Loyalty amongst Brothers

When David Miliband first went to visit Citizens UK, he must have done a double take. The organisation's small, non-descript office sits on Cavell Street, which is itself a dirty, non-descript side road off Whitechapel High Street in the East End of London. Litter skates across the pavements outside. Squashed plastic bottles, run over by chugging buses at the bus stop opposite, mix with cigarette butts. Signs of the fruit and vegetable market next door are everywhere. Cardboard boxes that once carried kiwis lie abandoned by the street's purple wheelie bins. Women in hijabs walk past the office doors talking into mobiles and carrying blue plastic bags full of aubergines and coriander. The neighbourhood is densely packed with tiny organisations, working hard and easy to miss. A money transfer stop, a women's sewing station, a small café. It's the same ground where George Lansbury, former Labour leader and community organiser in the 1930s, used to go about his work campaigning for social justice, supporting the dockers in their famous strike in 1889 for a better wage. The faces in London's East End might be a lot more diverse than in Lansbury's time, but he was still held up as an inspiration by Glasman and his colleagues, who saw Citizens UK as continuing in his tradition.

David Miliband and his team arrived at the East London office in the spring of 2010 and were quickly ushered into Citizens UK's main meeting room. The large room's grey carpet still has prints of the footsteps of organisers and community leaders traipsing in and out. It's clean and functional, but there is a faint lingering smell of hoovered carpets and office kitchens; an undertone of coffee and stale milk. A well-used pine table sits in the centre of the room. On one wall there is a giant map of London covered with pins labeling the organisation's member institutions, on the other there is a worn whiteboard. Piles of papers sit in corners and newspaper cuttings and Citizens UK posters brand the walls. Photos of past Citizen UK's events and campaigns are framed everywhere. After the assembly in Methodist Central Hall, the faces of Gordon Brown, David Cameron and Nick Clegg speaking on their platforms were also put up, symbolising the most high profile moment in the organisation's history. A cheap, white, plastic clock ticks at the head of the room. Citizens UK's organisers are sharp timekeepers, and that day they – like David Miliband – meant business.

This meeting would be the beginning of what became known as the "Movement for Change" (M4C) campaign. The idea was to contract Citizens UK to help train Labour party supporters in their organising techniques throughout the summer of the election campaign. It was an unconventional idea to say the least, and it was no secret that David Miliband was in two minds when he first entered this room. He got Citizens UK in theory, but he knew very little about their practice. He was there because he respected James Purnell, his former colleague in cabinet, and his chief political officer Madlin Sadler. Together they had persuaded him that this organisation could enrich his leadership campaign and address the future needs of the Labour party, which he had long believed was in need of significant regeneration. David Miliband knew that his closest confidantes were impressed by this organisation, and he also knew that it was connected to Brown's mysterious speech that had given unexpected life to Labour's general election campaign. He was here to give it a try, but it was still unknown. The office at Citizens UK must have felt a long way from the office of foreign secretary. A man with charisma and confidence in the highest power circles was now entering a very different world.

One of the chief sources of his unease was Maurice Glasman. Although never once billed as a Blue Labour project, David Miliband must not have been able to escape the knowledge that the real catalyst behind this meeting was Glasman. It was this scruffy academic who first introduced Purnell to Citizens UK and their training programmes. It was Glasman who had been dropping hints around his Labour friends about the need for a community organising body in the party and it was Glasman who had brokered this meeting with him and Neil Jameson, head of Citizens UK now. The fact that this link was made by a man he still remained suspicious of can't have helped matters. Purnell he could trust; but Purnell's trust in Glasman he was still unsure about. Leaving aside Glasman's critique of New Labour, the academic had still not come out for David Miliband's campaign.

Few people knew that Glasman had a personal connection with Ed Miliband after the two had worked together on the Citizens UK assembly, or that Glasman had given Ed Miliband the flagship policy for his campaign; the commitment to the living wage. This was also the chief campaign of the organisation that David Miliband was visiting now. When David Miliband walked through the doors of Citizens UK's building, he can't have failed to notice the living wage posters that lined the walls. Even though the Labour party collectively endorsed the Living Wage under Gordon Brown in the 2010 manifesto, it would have been hard not to see it as a sign of division. Glasman had encouraged Ed Miliband to take on the living wage campaign; now he was promoting Citizens UK organising techniques to David Miliband. Ed Miliband had chosen the campaign to constrain the market; his brother was taking the campaign to build community. Ed Miliband had chosen a tangible policy, David Miliband had taken the organising system behind it. Whether this was by chance or symptomatic of some set of personality traits within the two brothers remains open. But the fact that Glasman continued to offer advice to both campaigns was a source of tension throughout the summer.

From the perspective of Citizens UK, the clash of cultures was also acute. They had never done anything like this before. Of course it was a phenomenal opportunity, but not everyone had thought it was a good idea. Due to its diverse membership, Citizens UK had always remained a strictly apolitical organisation. Now they had been approached with a bid from a political party. Although the contract would go to a newly established social enterprise branch of the organisation – the Centre for Civil Society – it was still a big decision. Everything was moving very quickly. Now that they had actually got David Miliband in the room, there were no guidelines or protocols about how they would function. There was only one way they knew how to operate: as organisers. They sat in a circle, and started their meeting as they always did, with an introduction about the personal motivations and life stories of those in attendance. One of the organisers in the room remembers there being an obvious divergence of styles from the start:

> Each person had two minutes to say "why they joined the Labour party". David said his motivation was feeling angry about Thatcher and Conservative politics in the 1980s. This was a story he was used to telling but it wasn't about David; they were public stories about policy. It was fascinating for us because we are so used to personal stories. David's team didn't know each other's stories and it seemed within the party relationships were built through action, action, action rather than giving the time and space to get to know each other.

This was not to say by any means that David Miliband was mechanical or wooden. There was a difference, according to Citizens UK, between being confident and charismatic and being "relational":

> David's very charming – he sits in a room and he's got gravitas, he can answer questions with eloquence and he's friendly and smiley. It's not difficult to get to know him on a surface level, very easy in fact, but it was much harder to get beneath that. When we first met him, he wasn't particularly "relational" but I saw that change.

Whether he felt awkward or not, David Miliband came out of that meeting deciding to take a chance. Citizens UK was awarded the contract to help train 1,000 Labour party supporters over the summer with funding from Lord Sainsbury. In addition to this, the organisers would work with David Miliband himself to develop his understanding of the organisation's techniques. This decision was the first step on a long journey, both a deeply personal one for David Miliband, and a highly political one for the party. By the end of the leadership contest, those working closest with David Miliband at Citizens UK believed that he had personally changed, if not transformed. Not only was he having to deal with the constant media spotlight and tense family relations with his brother, he'd also committed to taking on an organisation that would push him to his limits in areas that this seemingly all-confident character may have been less comfortable. It was a journey that challenged the idea that he was just an ambitious but orthodox politician that only talked about policy with a capital P. By the end of his experiment with a new form of politics in September, he would relate to people on a personal level by publicly sharing more about himself.

This, then, was the beginning of an important and under-reported part of David Miliband's campaign. It was also set to be a historic moment for the Labour party. In shaking up how the party did politics from the bottom up, this was a radical experiment that would challenge the status quo. By letting Citizens UK into Labour's local constituency and branch parties, the Movement for Change undercut members who had performed these roles for generations. It demonstrated a fundamentally different way of doing things.

It would disrupt established power hierarchies and cause a clash of cultures on the ground and in David Miliband's office. Some of these systems were decaying, others were still powerful – many were resistant. A man with any less stature in the party – or any less funding – could probably not have pulled off such a risky move in the time frame available. David Miliband hoped it would end with him becoming leader of the party, and expected he could then carry on the movement at the helm.

The problem

David Miliband had identified a set of problems in the party that had long been swept under the carpet by his colleagues in government. The problems centred around party members; their recruitment, role and development. At the bottom end of the party chain, there had been a hemorrhaging of members for some time. Worse than that, the members that were there were becoming less loyal or losing interest. Britain was entering a new stage common across the industrialised world where party loyalty was not something born into by birth, but a consumer choice that was liable to change. Although there had been a wave of new members coming in after the election in fury at the Liberal Democrats, everyone knew these numbers were liable to change with the political tide. New recruits came from a different generation. They were mostly young, who were used to engagement, social media and participation. In many areas across the country, the local branch structures in place were left over from the war years and before; they were hierarchical, top down and bureaucratic. The new members were clashing with the old structures. In a report spearheaded by Will Straw and others over the summer called Labour Values, the group recognised that many existing members were ashamed to bring their newly signed up members to branch meetings lest they be put off the party altogether by boredom and bureaucracy. Many branches were struggling to be quorate, whilst others were dominated by long-standing members who had a vested interest in the status quo. Although many constituency parties were doing fantastic work, that was often by lottery than design. David Miliband could see the hollowing out of constituencies in traditional urban strongholds where membership was falling, and as a strategic thinker he was worried about what might happen in other cities ten years ahead. As Purnell put it:

> reconstituting the party was always his [David Miliband's] thing... community organising was the solution to which he had identified the problem, so one of his things was always about reorganising the party and I think Madlin [Sadler] and I both thought that community organising would be a good way of doing that. I think there was also something about New Labour originally which was all about going to talk to all the Labour Party members. There had been quite a strong dominance of people running the Labour Party in the 80's and of course when you went to talk to Labour party members that wasn't what they thought at all so... community organising I think is a way of demonstrating a way of evolving New Labour ideas but it's also a way of demonstrating that those who have got strong roots in lots of Labour party traditions.

For Purnell then, the aim of introducing organising to Citizens UK wasn't just about reconnecting to the distant Labour tradition of organising before 1945, it was also about going back to the glory days of New Labour, when it was still new with a small "n". Purnell saw the emergence of Tony Blair and New Labour as reconnecting with people's genuine concerns. It might also bypass the "gatekeepers" of member opinion – more radical branch chairs and union interests – who tended to give a skewed perspective of what members actually wanted. New Labour had originally managed this; it was only after coming to government that things went astray. If done well, Purnell believed organising wasn't just a way of reorganising party structures, but also reconnecting with the values of British people that might shape Labour's future agenda:

I would conceptualise it as going back to New Labour to Sedgefield in 1994. Tony in the late 80's, 90's first came to prominence for having 1600 people in his local party then being massively active having lots of barbecues and you know in the 80's the Labour party had been at risk, but also had its ideas led by a much more liberal bit of the Labour party and what Tony, and Gordon and Peter were about was saying the reason we have lost, they were saying crime affects ordinary working people, ordinary working people think that others should work if they get the chance to do so, it was saying that people wanted good public service, it was about minimum wage and 4 weeks paid leave. I think probably what Maurice would say would be that New Labour then lost a lot of that over the next 15 years, I wouldn't totally agree with him but he would certainly say that. That method of organising brings you in touch with what people are afraid of and what they can do together to make their lives better.

The Movement for Change was brilliantly targeted because it suited the few interests at the top that mattered. For David Miliband it was a short-term way of making an impact that would demonstrate his character and leadership, which could get him known as having some original ideas if not get him direct votes. For Purnell it was about all of this, and reconnecting with the values and ideas of British people. Both men also seemed genuinely intrigued by this organisation's potential. For Glasman, it was about pushing his ideas about community organising and reconfiguring the party to the centre stage of the leadership battle and the heart of the Labour party. For Citizens UK, it was a chance to earn some money and raise their profile even further by tying their brand to who they must have believed was the most likely future Labour leader, and the potential prime minister of the country. In short, Movement for Change might have been an attempt to regenerate the grassroots, but it originated in a pact of overlapping interests right at the very top of the party.

The politics of practice

The idea was simple. In the four months until the votes were cast, the Movement for Change campaign would aim to train 1,000 Labour activists in community organising techniques to go on and serve the party. Using a generous grant from Lord Sainsbury, two Citizens UK activists would be seconded from the London office for the summer and run programmes all over the country. They would form an autonomous unit within the David Miliband campaign, open to members and non-members. With limited space and resources, they would run actions up and down the country on the back of the training. By the conference in September, they wanted to have a bank of successful case studies to showcase to the rest of the party. The training would all be Citizens UK style, and would provide another way of doing things. Individuals would be trained whether they were official Labour members or David Miliband supporters or not to show the party that this was more than just an election strategy; it was a commitment to the long-term interests of the Labour party. The intention was to demonstrate that David Miliband had personality and vision. Importantly, it was a commitment that marked him out without – unlike the living wage – having to make any declarations about increases in public spending or holding difficult negotiations with big business. If he won, it would serve as an experiment for a new way of doing things under his leadership. If he didn't win, it would at least prove to be a useful experiment. The potential cultural change was immense. The fact that David Miliband failed to fully convey the scale of the ambition suggests perhaps he still had some doubts about its significance.

When Jonathan Cox, 29, found out that he was going to be seconded to work on David's team, he almost fell off his pew. He found out via text message whilst holding a meeting with a community leader at a church in Battersea. It came from the head of Citizens UK, and it simply said: "How would you feel about introducing community organising to the Labour Party as part of David Miliband's leadership campaign?". A young organiser from South Wales, Cox was a small, neat man with glasses. The son of a vicar and a college lecturer, he was a quiet but sharp organiser who had been running the Citizens for Sanctuary campaign, which had pushed David Cameron and Nick Clegg to end the detention of children for immigration purposes. He was chosen partly on efficiency and his ability to deliver, and because he had some connection with the Labour party, having formerly worked for a Labour MP. After very few meetings, Cox quickly discovered that if he wanted to make the headway necessary, he would need extra help. Enter Sophie Stephens, a young Oxbridge graduate, and George Gabriel, both young and dedicated organisers with a record of delivering results.

Between the three of them, Stephens, Gabriel and Cox had to come up with a plan that would fill the four months. They would work almost entirely alone. They started doing taster plans in the areas that they were recommended. Although working across a diverse geographical area – Manchester, Wales, Leeds and other areas as well as London – they were often areas recommended by the party that were Labour strongholds. This later came up as an issue when the party was looking at replication. A deliberate attempt was also made to find members who weren't necessarily already plugged into their local branch structures. Interested individuals could sign up via email on David Miliband's campaign site, and further interest was generated through David Miliband's personal campaign emails, which invited people to join. By going over the heads of the local branches, the Movement for Change had the advantage of reaching people they had never worked with before, but had the disadvantage of occasionally irritating the local powers that be.

When the organisers sifted through those that contacted them, they applied their normal strategy of looking for spark or talent – people they thought could be leaders in the community and get turn-out. Citizens UK was always quite ruthless about finding and working with the players that were going to get things done – often tied to community groups and institutions – and ditching the rest. It was an effective if not an entirely inclusive strategy. Through that contact, they would chase their networks to meet other community members. They would then run a "listening campaign" in that area, knocking on doors trying to figure out what issues local people felt needed addressing. Once they hit on common ground for action, they would try to fix it. With the September deadline looming ahead of them, small pockets of action started springing up all over. There were several successful examples that often get cited by the campaign. In one area of Manchester for example a group of residents founded the "Northern Moore Community Respect Covenant". Started by an organiser knocking on the door with one Labour party member and asking what they cared about, they discovered it was breakdown of relationships in the community and crime and anti-social behaviour. A bit more door knocking got together a rally in the Manchester drizzle of some 50 people, bringing down an MP and local councillor to sign a covenant of respect. The local police team came down and agreed to do more shifts and the profile of the area was raised. In an area of Nottingham, the big issue was street lighting. The local council was planning to cut public street lights, leaving the town in darkness for the first time since the 1800s. Gabriel helped run a massive campaign to save the lights, gathering the community together under a dark tunnel one night and filling it with fairy lights. It became a high profile campaign in the community, and the lights were saved.

Whilst all this was happening on the ground, the organisers were also keen to work on David Miliband himself. The chief means for doing this was through an organising technique known as a "one to one" (1-2-1). A one to one is an intimate meeting where two people discuss their personal motivations for political involvement in an attempt to build working relationships. Organisers hold David Miliband in high esteem for being prepared to participate in such meetings, albeit a little gingerly at first. Cox said they were deliberately trying to set up one to ones for David Miliband with "ordinary people" to help him open up and understand their experiences, but in the heat of the election campaign, they didn't always go to plan:

> We saw a big change over the course of the campaign – from amiability and charm to moving beyond that to becoming much more relational… The first one to one David did was with a teacher, mother to a young kid, living in the city, struggling with the same issues that ordinary people everywhere are struggling with, and she was disillusioned with Labour – she was not a member, David did a one to one with her, and this is a classic thing that is symptomatic of the frustration – because there were some people organising his diary at the time who didn't get the one to one thing and so we kept saying: "Look you have to give us time to train him how to do these, they need a minimum of 45 minutes for each one, and it needs to be in a quiet place where they can relax and be comfortable. What happened was that his visit overran and he ended up

doing the one to one for 25 minutes in the back of his car on the way to the station and, you know, it's hard to relate to people effectively in that sort of environment. I spoke to the lady afterwards, asking her how it went and she said he was very polite and charming and genuinely listened, it was a fantastic opportunity to meet him etc. but that because of the time and his natural preference for talking about policy, she didn't feel there was any kind of deep engagement or relationship there – which is the point of the one to one. That was the start – and as he did more of these one to ones, behind closed doors with ordinary people, he got much better at them.

The problem seemed to be, as Glasman would later say in an interview with the *Times*, that David Miliband was not relational. Around journalists and other politicians he was charismatic, charming and eloquent. This was the man who had charmed Hillary Clinton as foreign secretary, and managed to win alliances around the world. But when it came to talking about personal issues – his motivations, hopes, fears and experiences – David Miliband was not on sure ground. Citizens UK was about getting the personal into politics. It was founded on trust and relationships. Without that insight and understanding into who he was, there could be no action. It was core principle of Citizens UK's philosophy that relationships underpinned political change. As Cox identified, given the situation with his brother, it was difficult for David Miliband to discuss intimate matters. But Cox was still pushing the leadership candidate to open up:

In a one to one we don't want to pry into people's private lives but we do want to know what is personal to them.

When Brown said, "I am a son of a Presbyterian preacher and you will always find in me a friend and a brother", that went down so well because he personally related to people in the room, he shared his personal story. The difficulty was he [David Miliband] was struggling to share that personal stuff because it was so linked to the private thing in his mind and he couldn't… that included Ed and his family. Actually when you saw him with people he was quite relational – he loves to talk about policy and politics. But this was the other challenge for us: getting him to relate to people as a personal figure, and again he got better at doing this over the course of time and discovered the value of it.

With these obstacles in mind, Cox, sat down with David Miliband to give him some personal training. Cox describes it as a clearly personal and revelatory moment:

There was another noticeable improvement when we had the opportunity to sit down with him and train him how to do effective one to ones. We sat down in his office and, you know, he was his usual charming and enthusiastic self. I just said "Look, I'm here and I want to do a one to one and give you some training and you need to learn to do this." And so we did it in the usual way – I shared a bit about myself in two minutes and I said "Tell me about you", and he said "What do you want to know?" and I said, "Well I want to know about you", and he said "You can read that on the website." I said "I want you to tell me, okay start with this, tell me why you are running to be leader of the Labour Party?" He was uncomfortable and said "You've seen all my statements you know all this." So I asked a deliberately agitational question to get him to open up, and said "Tell me, I've worked with you for a few weeks now and I have seen you at your most human at your most real, I've seen you smile most when you have been with your family, and you are a different person. Tell me this, you have spent three years as foreign secretary or whatever, the past thirteen years you have given your life to the Labour project, you love your kids and wife, they are growing up, Labour aren't going to win the next election, and instead of spending time with your family you are now spending every evening this summer going to a ridiculous number of meetings around the country to try and vote you in, why are you doing that? And he said "Because life is an adventure." I was like "What?! That doesn't sound like an adventure to me, and that doesn't tell me why you are doing it. Tell me." He said, "Well I guess if you really want to know the reason I do this, the reason I'm willing to sacrifice that time – which you are right, I could be spending with my family, who I love and do want to spend more time with – the reason I think this is really important to do and the reason it is important comes from something taught to me by my father. If you have a gift, talent and vision and you choose not to use it then that is a crime. When I grew up the Holocaust seemed quite recent growing up in a Jewish family where many of our relatives had been killed in the Holocaust – it might be really distant for you but when I was growing up that was still pretty real for us and we were strongly taught by my father that if you had a talent and you had the opportunity to use it then you should use it for the common good, and that is the reason I was doing the job." I said, "Why aren't you telling the people you want to vote for you this story?" And he said, "My brother has used the same story already." After this he got more comfortable with the one to ones and the relationships seemed to energise his campaigning and his natural amiability moved into his becoming more relational.

None of this was unique to David Miliband. Most organisers admitted that this was something to do with political life. As Purnell said, it was "not easy to be relational in politics", when you have to be on your guard and time is always scarce. If David Miliband was more "non-relational" than most, he was also one of the few politicians with the courage to try it. Throughout the campaign, David Miliband would participate in one to ones to develop his ability to relate to a range of people outside Westminster. In one particular session with a young Iranian, Purnell said David Miliband came out "full of enthusiasm and energy". Intentional or not, Movement for Change had the effect of making him talk to ordinary people and open up to them in a way that had become closed when he was foreign secretary. By the end of the summer, organisers who had initially felt a coolness towards him had developed an affection for the man they had come to see as their candidate.

Clash of cultures

Critics and supporters of David Miliband have offered many reasons as to why he failed to become Labour leader. One of the overlooked reasons is the failure of his team and its candidate to decide fully whether to fight a conventional campaign or one that placed a new form of community politics at its centre. Not everyone in David Miliband's office felt that the Movement for Change was a good idea. For those running

David Miliband's overall campaign in the office behind the scenes – the people managing his media appearances, his diary and his overall strategy – this was a rather quirky risk. From their perspective, there were three problems with it.

First, it wasn't obvious how this was going to translate into actual votes for the leadership election. It was not, as they were used to doing, direct canvassing of voters and MPs. It was not telephone banking or ticking people off a list or schmoozing media contacts. As Cox later put it, they'd never been asked to do the "Obama thing". The point, for better or worse, was genuinely to do some organising in the party. This would have been fine, it hadn't been for the second problem: opportunity cost. As one field organiser who didn't want to be identified put it: "it was a giant waste of money". The Movement for Change wasn't just expensive – it also took up essential time from David Miliband's diary. Rather than courting the powers that be at the top, he was visiting small houses and streets up and down the country and talking to them about street lighting and their problems with local corner shops. On top of that, the Labour supporters being trained didn't have to be signed up members of David Miliband's campaign or even the Labour party to partici-pate – that meant they might not even be able to vote in September.

Finally, Movement for Change conflicted with his central campaign office's power base. David Miliband was suddenly divided; he couldn't always go where they told him to. The Movement for Change was semi-autonomous, they had little control over it, but it had the commitment of the leader behind it and could therefore make demands on his time. Cox, Gabriel and Stephens were all in their twenties, and had no experience of political campaigning. To the heavy-weights in David Miliband's office, they must have looked more than a little naïve. Now they were having to fight for David Miliband's time with them. As Cox put it:

> when we did Movement for Change there was huge appetite for it among senior figures in the party, amongst David and James Purnell and some of the people who have been in the party a long time and at high level and so on. There was huge appetite for it at grassroots level from Labour Party members, particularly many Labour Party members who had not been active before. There was real resistance, as there is whenever there is organisational change, from those who already had some stake in the status quo and felt a little threatened by this. So that included people on the campaign, some who thought this was a good idea but the wrong time to do it, which could be a well justified point. They initially saw Movement for Change as a distraction from winning the campaign, and said things like: "what you are doing is absolutely the right thing – let's do it after we win the election". So there was a bit of that. There were a few people who thought this community organising thing was verging on cultish, too heavily linked to faith and we shouldn't have any truck with it and they were always unhappy with it. There were other people who may have really liked the ideas if it didn't threaten them, like some councillors, or MPs, although, to be fair, there were not many.

This clash of cultures manifested itself in the smallest things. At a very simple level, organisers had their language of one to ones, leaders and house meetings. Politicians had their own jargon centred around voters and people turn-out.

When organising an event, David Miliband's team's approach was to blanket email everyone they had the contact details for whether they knew them or not, and hope that one hundred would turn up. Citizen UK's approach was to work from relationships, personally calling the ten people they knew and getting them each to bring the ten that they knew. At an event, an important part of Citizen UK's approach was audience participation, not just in terms of content but also helping to run the ceremonies. It was important for their members to leave feeling that they had a fun time as well as an informative one. This was less of a concern for the members of David Miliband's campaign, who were more likely to run a traditional event with a strong divide between speaker and audience. Even an unscripted Q&A was a bit of a risk. As Stephens put it:

> David's campaign were helpful and very kind. However, we understood there was tension over what this would deliver in terms of votes, pure votes. We were all asking how do we translate community organising into electoral politics? Some people were really supportive, they knew we were out organising – going around the country meeting and training community leaders and local party members. Others liked our work, but felt it should happen after the election. But for us it needed to happen during the leadership campaign because that period of energy and optimism meant that people were actually committed to trying something new. We needed that.

But the Movement for Change organisers weren't just treading on the toes of those inside David Miliband's campaign team. They were also causing tensions in the wider Labour party.

It was all very well trying out a new method of campaigning, but the Movement for Change campaign was parachuting into areas that had their own pre-existing organisations, hierarchies and set ways of doing things. Labour has hundreds of local branches run by members all over the country, many of which are fiercely territorial and have a strong sense of local accountability. David Miliband's team may have only been going to areas where Labour had some sort of presence, but inevitably that area would have its own local branch structures, councillors and members. There was no guarantee that they would all be David Miliband supporters, let alone be prepared to sign up to the Movement for Change. Although the team only went where they were invited, there were plenty of vested interests to tread on. In the time scale available, it wasn't possible to inform all of the relevant interests when they were coming or what they were doing. For those that weren't told, it must have looked like David Miliband's army were parking up on their own back lawn, and it shook things up. For others it must have felt as if they were being insulted. The way they were running things can't have been good enough, otherwise David Miliband's team wouldn't have felt the need to send someone in. As Cox put it:

> we only went where we were invited and we made sure there was the local gatekeeper, someone there local, a senior MP, candidate or whatever. But power, of course, is not all vested in one person – just because the MP invites us in doesn't mean the constituency chair likes it, and doesn't mean the secretary likes it.

In one particular example, the Movement for Change

team visited Brynmawr, a small Welsh town. The team decided to do a "neighbourhood walk", a basic tour through the community to talk to residents and get to know what issues were affecting them. But even this small action caused quite a lot of complaints, as Cox explains:

> [the walk] caused a real tension because one of the CLP officers was like "What's going on here" and he got in touch with the MP and made a complaint and the whole thing was "We have a structure here and everything must go through the structure and unless I say this is okay this is not going to happen", which is of course completely counter to the culture that we are trying to encourage, which is one where people talk to each other, they are relational, you don't have someone preventing someone from doing something which is perfectly reasonable.

Nor were these problems self-contained. They would often come back to haunt the Movement for Change team as complaints went straight to the top:

> whoever was dissatisfied would go back to someone else in David's team who was arranging the visit for David and say it's causing problems and those people would say Movement for Change is causing problems here, and it didn't help that some people in the team were not particularly keen on what we were doing.

The Citizens UK approach to organising was designed to take on established power structures and find a way to make them change when other measures had failed. The problem was that in party politics, the power that often refused to budge might well be fellow party members – a local Labour MP, a Labour leader of a council or a local business with strong connections to their local Labour politicians. So when the vice-chair of Enfield CLP decided to take on the issue of estate doors being broken with the Movement for Change campaign, he had to take on the leader of his local council, who was not just a Labour colleague, but a friend. The cause was a worthy one – many residents had been left feeling unsafe in their own homes – but the means trod on toes. With the help of the CLP vice chair and Movement for Change organisers, one hundred local people signed a petition that was delivered to the council. In the end the result was successful; the council caved in and got the doors fixed, but as one organiser said, "it was not an easy journey for anyone". For a campaign founded on relationships, the Movement for Change trod on a few.

Nor did the objections just come from stuffy bureaucrats and vested power interests. Some of the most vocal criticisms came from Labour activists dedicated to community work. Some questioned how proper relationships could be built in such a small space of time, when there was so much pressure on the players to deliver action and results for the David Miliband campaign. Others cared genuinely about the issues, but were afraid of being tied to what was very much perceived as the "David Miliband camp". The officials at David Miliband HQ might have been worried that this was not close enough to David Miliband's campaign, but those who were interested in getting involved for the sake of community were still wary that they might simply become foot soldiers in a new 1,000 strong David Miliband army. Others worried what would happen after the leadership campaign – there was a fear that irrespective of the result, the end of the campaign might mean the Movement for Change would fizzle out.

But it would be over simplistic to characterise the Movement for Change as solely a source of conflict. Whether you agree with it or not, change is always a difficult process when traditional hierarchies are at stake. By the end of the campaign, Citizens UK organisers did manage to win some people around. One member of David Miliband's campaign – who didn't want to be named – said that despite an initial scepticism of the Movement for Change, they came to see its advantages:

> Although I was initially suspicious, I came to see its advantages. The old system of party organisation with its traditional hierarchical structures had less power and relevance in a world where they couldn't act as gatekeepers for information, so bringing in another body didn't make that much difference. Of course it would irritate some of the old guard, but it was also appealing to a younger generation that felt isolated from the traditional way of doing things.

When asked about the challenges of M4C in his campaign, David Miliband acknowledged that there was an "electricity" involved in renewing politics, but denied there was any fundamental tension.

The shard of Glasman

Meanwhile back at base camp, Glasman was causing

problems. He might have been personally responsible for seeding the Movement for Change campaign, but he was still unwilling to throw his cards in with it completely. Throughout the campaign, Glasman said he was very open about the fact that he was not going to "take sides in a family argument". He would have regular meetings with the inner core of David Miliband's campaign, but he continued to talk to Ed Miliband's team. In what he described as a "long and difficult summer" Glasman admitted he came under pressure to come down on one side or the other by both brothers.

On a purely personal level, Glasman clicked better with Ed Miliband. The pair had a more emotional connection, and Glasman said he related to him as they were both younger brothers, and because they had achieved things together. Perhaps more importantly, Glasman was convinced that Ed Miliband was going to win. Right from the start, even before the polls were indicating otherwise, he said he thought that Ed Miliband had "more energy" than his older brother.

But on the other side, Glasman had a more close personal relationship with David Miliband's team. He might not have clicked with David Miliband himself, but Purnell and Cruddas were some of his closest friends, and they had made Movement for Change happen. On top of that, Glasman had serious concerns with the way Ed Miliband was running his campaign, particularly with the unions. In something of a paradox, Glasman told Ed Miliband to challenge his perceived closeness with the unions whilst telling David Miliband to strike a deal with them. Cox later acknowledged that Glasman's role was ambiguous to say the least:

Maurice was around but not around, he never worked for

David's campaigns, he helped him with a couple of speeches and then was just hovering and was there occasionally to give advice and direction, but he's never really done a huge amount of direct organising on the ground and has never been a professional organiser, so he left us to it basically. There was a little advisory team which included him and James Purnell and others who helped us out enormously every month or so, but then it was down to us.

But it would be over simplistic to dismiss Glasman as simply ruthlessly self-interested. Talk to Glasman himself, and he seems genuinely tortured by his behaviour during those months. For a man who talked about the importance of relationships, he seemed genuinely concerned about messing them up, and was agonising about his own inability to commit either way. From May to September, Glasman kept flitting between the two campaigns, unable to decide between the two brothers and constantly wondering whether to "pack it all in and write a book". There may have been a slight love of the drama, but his descriptions of the summer seem to convey a genuine sense of tension, and at one point he did leave for a holiday in Sardinia. Even friends of Glasman – who wished to remain anonymous – suggested he exhibited an element of naivety during the contest, but believed that the conflict was genuine.

Keeping a foot in both camps might look strategic with hindsight, but at the time Glasman was playing a dangerous game. Walking a tight-rope between the two brothers, he could have been pushed off by either side at any time. The stakes were high. Keeping a connection in both camps gave Glasman the possibility of having a connection with the leader of the Labour party whoever won the campaign. But it also ran the risk of pushing both of them away and being left with nothing. Listen to Glasman talk, and the tension is clear. It is hard to imagine such a combination of genius, naivety, love and power, loyalty and self interest:

Why was it so difficult for you to choose between the two brothers?

I really loved the relationship that I had with Ed, that was all built around action, and doing things and he did them. So I had a long and very difficult summer, I worked closely with David, but I also worked with Ed, I wrote a piece for the *New Statesman*, saying roughly that David hadn't had a proper reckoning with Blair and Ed hadn't had a proper reckoning with Brown and neither represented a transformative agenda but that was just me trying to get out of making a choice, I wanted to keep my relationship with James and Jon, that was hugely important to me, but I also wanted to keep my relationship with Ed who I liked a lot, not a big fan of his campaign. So that's where I was.

Did either side pressure you to come down one way or another?

Oh yes.

How did you respond to that?

I would just say I haven't come this far in my life to take sides in a family argument, that I wasn't going to do that, and but I wanted to keep my relationship with both. It was a tricky summer keeping relationships with both sides and in a way I could justify it, self servingly, by, I had an idea and I was interested in developing the idea within Labour, and it was important that it transcended divisions. I also unbelievably spoke with Diane Abbot bearing in mind where she is at the moment, had a conversation with her... in the end I just went on holiday, I went to Sardinia, it was the first holiday family in five years and I didn't know what to do, and I just said alright, I'll write a book, I've made friends, I'll keep working. So I sort of came back and really spoke to Ed about where I was and just said "Look I really like you, I think you can do it." I had the conversation about six weeks before maybe, August, beginning of August. But I kept working with James, Jon, on David's side and talking to Ed and both sides knew, it wasn't a secret I was engaged with both. I wrote a speech for David called the Keir Hardie speech, I didn't think it led to a genuine transformation of his agenda, so you know, tricky. I know that some people think I played some kind of pre-conceived hand but really I was just pretty distressed by the relationship between them, the fact there was very little to choose in many ways, and above all that I was attracted to Ed emotionally, and pulled to David through relationships – as I like to write "humph", that was where I was.

What did Ed Miliband see in you, and what did David Miliband see in you?

What David saw in me was he really liked James, he was really interested in Jon as an ally, and I worked closely with both and then I really think David really began to understand the organising agenda which was incredible, but he did, he began to get it, that actually talking to people. I remember the first time we spoke and he said what does organising mean, let's have a chat I said "Why did you go into politics?" and he went … [expression] "What?" Well that's it, that's all you have to do, tell the whole story and listen to people and see where you are, and he really supported Movement for Change and had continued to do so and that is to his great honour. Whereas Ed, really kind of got the language, the rebelliousness of it, and he also, I feel got a kind of a sense of where people are at, Ed likes people and he likes to be loved by people, and he understood that in the Blue Labour story of engaging with where people are.

How did Ed Miliband see you?

As someone who had worked in organising, who could write speeches, who could be a real… and as I said to him, Ed, I'm stuck in a set of genuine friendships that means I can't come out for you, and I can't come out for David, because I want the relationships I have got plus your campaign isn't really doing it, you know, with Neil Kinnock, and the unions, these are all things that have to be confronted down the road. .

Someone told me they felt that Ed and David Miliband both saw you as an uncle figure, someone who provided emotional support. Do you think there is any truth in that?

Well I don't know how they, sometimes it's hard for me to conceptualise myself, I'm not, I never took a psychoanalytic view, it's possible, you know, I'm older than them, I've had more experience of life it was good, you know, I felt more a connection to Ed, to be honest, but I would say it was a much more equal thing than an uncle thing, we would basically sit and argue with each other.

How did you feel being stuck in the middle?

I felt I'd completely fucked it, you know, I hadn't built a really strong relationship with either to be truthful, I didn't support David, I really felt strongly for Ed, that couldn't come out, I didn't like the campaign. I remember on holiday talking to Catherine saying this has all been great, I've learnt a lot, once again go home write a book, go back to organising was one of the thoughts.

Who did you think would win?

I was convinced that Ed would win from the start, because he had the energy.

But you didn't like his campaign?

I didn't think he asked the hard questions to the party, right now there is going to have to be a huge change in the unions to bring them into a much more constructive relationship for the good, there is going to have to be a big change in the party organisation to bring it closer to people, there is going to have to be a big change in welfare, so build an all round responsibility, contribution... there is going to have to have a very strong private sector growth because there is no real jobs for the people and we're going to have to think about that.

And you thought David Miliband got that side of it more?

No, he didn't particularly, he got the organising more, but he was still in the financial sector, you know, he was still, I felt that David was still imprisoned by a Blairite prison and I thought that essentially Ed was still working within a Brownite one, he was appealing to the unions, I loved the living wage but the living wage never caught fire, you know, he never did any living wage action, I used to say to Ed lets go to a bank, lets go to a local hospital and make a living wage Campaign, you know as part of your leadership and he strangely seemed reluctant to do that. So I didn't think a big message of transformation of change was coming out of Ed's campaign although he had it and I knew that. But I thought Ed would win first of all because he would appeal more to the party, but secondly because he had more energy to him, so I kept saying to David's lot I think Ed is going to win, and they didn't think he would. I remember saying to David that he should make an offer to the unions if he wanted to win, a constructive offer, but he didn't.

So I'm still struggling to understand why you couldn't put your cards in one camp. Are you saying it was purely because you were friends with Ed Miliband, but you were also friends with key players in David Miliband's team like Jon Cruddas and James Purnell?

Purely, and I just, the most important thing to me, as I was new to this was to keep the friendships I had, and I didn't, and I valued them, that's it.

Of course it would not be right to over exaggerate the significance of Glasman's ambiguity towards the leadership candidates. Glasman's dilemma might have meant the world to Glasman, but both Milibands had many other considerations on their minds as they sought the support of key labour and media figures. Both worked extremely hard to secure the support of newspaper editors, with Ed Miliband contacting at least one while they were on holiday in the hope of gaining an endorsement. But Glasman's indecision was significant in the sense that it was personal. He had come to be a known figure to them both. Glasman's agonising became part of the emotional and ideological intensity that marked a divide between two brothers and a party.

It wasn't as if Glasman was just playing a peripheral role in David Miliband's campaign either. Every few weeks, Glasman would join an important meeting with David Miliband and his core Movement for Change team – Sadler, Purnell, Cox and Stephens – to discuss how the campaign was going. Here was where the tension was really felt. In his usual frank style, Glasman would point out what he saw were the problems with the campaign, whilst being very open about the fact that he was continuing to see Ed. Glasman's strongest problem was David Miliband's weak relationship with the unions, which he identified – somewhat prophetically – as the Achilles heel of the campaign. As Purnell remembers the meetings:

Maurice is being fairly candid in those meetings because one of the things community organising teaches you is not to shy away from conflict, that conflict is good, he was telling David pretty openly what he thought the problems were with the campaign.

Although there was clearly tension between the two, Purnell said that David Miliband did take "some of it (Glasman's advice) on board". In perhaps the strongest example of collaboration, David Miliband committed to delivering a speech that Glasman had written. Made on July 9th in Wales, the "Keir Hardie" speech was written by Glasman with the help of Cruddas and spoke directly to Blue Labour ideals. In the speech itself, Glasman drew on the traditions of Keir Hardie, the Scottish socialist who served as Labour's first independent member of parliament in the early 1900s. Like Brown's speech, this was one that stood out in the campaign and was referenced and downloaded many times. Leaving aside a few exceptions like Ed Balls' Bloomberg speech, this contribution from David Miliband left the others look bland.

The August assembly

The original plan for Movement for Change had been to spend four months training activists in community organising to build towards a grand assembly in September. The plan was to showcase the best projects in what the organisers hoped would coincide with David Miliband's coronation. But the organisers of the Movement for Change campaign quickly realised that there were three key problems with leaving it so late. The first was votes. A ceremony at the end of the campaign might be inspirational, but it would be too late to give anyone a chance to change their preferences on the ballot. Holding an event earlier might help generate press coverage at a time when it was proving difficult to sustain media interest. Second, from the tension inside David Miliband's campaign, it was obvious that they needed to demonstrate their value. Helping the team win votes was clearly the best way to do that. Finally, the assembly would also answer concerns from those individuals who had been engaged in the Movement for Change, but were worried about its sustainability and moral purpose. An assembly would give them a chance to hear from the man himself that he was committed to party rejuvenation – a difficult decision to go back on publicly.

So the decision was taken to hold another assembly, similar to the one planned in September, but a month earlier with 1,000 people in central London. It was a tall order. Cox had gone away for a month, so Stephens was left to organise it all with Gabriel. Working with an entirely new set of people, they had the challenge of packing out the hall and putting together an agenda with people they had only been working with for a period of weeks. Invitees had not been "tested" when it came to turn-out, and the entire strategy was high risk. If it went wrong, the Movement for Change would be brought into disrepute. They had to prove that it could deliver.

The event itself, held in the August of 2010, was a confluence of all the tensions and energy of the campaign so far. It was held in the Emmanuelle Centre, right by Westminster. Modelled on the traditional Citizens UK assembly, the presentations would come from the participants themselves. They would showcase the results they had achieved so far and put the politician – in this case David Miliband – on the spot by asking him what would happen to Movement for Change if he lost. On the back of this, David Miliband was set to give a seminal speech. According to Stephens, they were hoping it would be a "game changer".

At 1pm, Stephens was starting to panic. Only a handful of her 1,000 activists had arrived, and David Miliband's team were also late. It was a bank holiday, and there were severe transport problems. When David Miliband's team did eventually arrive 90 minutes before it was set to start, Stephens showed them the schedule, and they had serious problems with it. It was the week after Ed Miliband had been chastised in the press for making perceived religious overtones in his campaign, and David Miliband's staff were jumpy – particularly given this unusual assembly was being held in a church. They told her that a religious symbol high above the stage had to be covered up with a flag. Stephens later conceded that some of the changes David Miliband's team asked for were justified. Seating David Miliband in the middle of the organisers rather than at the side of them, for example, made sense for the photographers. Again, the problem came down to a clash of cultures. Citizens UK was used to putting the politician in an awkward position and "pinning" them on a set of demands, not flattering them with centre stage. Changes like this were understandable, but one organiser said that David Miliband's team were insisting on other changes that seemed less necessary:

> David's team arrived just before the start, read through the
> script and realised just how much this assembly was outside of

their comfort zone – some people tried to make last minute changes. Ed Miliband had been labelled as a preacher the week before and there was a real worry about how David would be seen. Stuff was worried about that didn't need to be worried about.

Then there was the issue of the speech. Glasman had written another testimony for David Miliband. A personal speech about David Miliband's story and values, it was supposed to be the high point of his campaign. The aim was to deliver a hit much like the one Brown had delivered in May. Glasman had been working on it, and the organisers were relying on his words to motivate the room and give a new injection of energy into the campaign. But David Miliband refused to read it. The speech that was supposed to bring him out into the world was left unread, and was never published. Glasman wanted David Miliband to go one way, he wanted to go another. This time David Miliband held his ground. He was coming to give a speech he felt more comfortable with. It was more personal, but it stuck to the line.

The assembly was supposed to be the turning point for David Miliband's profile and the campaign. It proved not to be so. But the organisers involved did say it was a turning point for David Miliband himself. When he did eventually enter the room, the entire hall was packed. It turned out the guests had arrived, they were just locked outside, and now that the full thousand had flooded in, he was met with huge and sustained applause. Stephens said afterwards that the room was not like the rooms David Miliband was used to giving speeches in. There was a highly diverse audience, with a massive range of community groups out in force and a whole rainbow of colours, ages and races represented. Half way through the assembly a Zimbabwean contingent spontaneously stood up and broke into song. These were not careerist politicians or spads in suits, they were community and faith groups from around the country. According to Stephens, their desired leader responded to that:

> David comes in to rapturous applause and at that moment David realised it changed. He'd come and met people involved in M4C before but he'd never seen it like this, not on this scale and not with this energy. I think then and there he realised that this was business and it really could work. It was so different to normal events – it was chaotic, funny, diverse and full of energy. He stood up and gave a great speech. It wasn't the May 3rd Brown speech but David seemed to speak from the heart because the people in that room were relating to him. I understand that in his job you don't want to talk about your personal life, everything he says is so closely scrutinised but it was what the party members needed so they could understand him. It may feel like motivations and personal experiences aren't relevant to the national agenda but it's what makes you real.

When David Miliband was asked on stage whether he would commit to supporting the Movement for Change after the leadership election whatever the outcome, he said yes. Individuals that had come to hear David Miliband speak but weren't members signed up to join the party. David Miliband's team were baffled, but also slightly in awe that the whole process, tinkering on the border with anarchy, had actually come off. According to the organisers, when David

Miliband left that night he left a personal note thanking them for their efforts. He signed off with a line that went down in Citizens UK folklore as the moment when a politician got it. It ended simply: "With respect, David".

Although the exact moment varies, sources close to David Miliband agreed that the Movement for Change altered him. Another lead organiser in the campaign, Cox, said that David Miliband "discovered the value" of relational politics over time. According to Purnell, one of David Miliband's closest friends and supporters over the summer, it was the series of one to ones that really made a difference:

> I think at first it's hard to get him to do one to ones and actually when he started doing it he loved them and I think one of the reasons this campaign was really motoring at the end was, I think there is something about being foreign secretary that takes you out of Britain at a very obvious level and doing the one to ones and being properly rooted in England in particular suddenly gave him a whole load of things to talk about.

One year on from the campaign, David Miliband agreed to talk about how the Movement for Change affected his politics and his beliefs. Although reluctant to relate any personal experience at first, he did respond when he heard that other organisers felt that he personally moved throughout the campaign:

Did the Movement for Change change you?

Yes. It turned me from thinking about government for the people to government by the people. Doing politics from the bottom up rather than the top down. It gave practical form to something that I talked a lot about in government, which is that if you want to make change you need three things: government leadership, institutional innovation – from private and public organisations – and mass mobilisation.

What about on a personal level?

Yes, that too. Every time you have a one-to-one it restores your faith in human nature. It's a profoundly uncynical way of developing politics.

What do you remember about one to ones?

That's the point about one to one interactions; you remember them. I remember them whether it was the mother talking about the challenges of caring for her daughter, or the student talking about their fears and hopes for the future or a troubled youngster facing challenges – they are all striking experiences that brought people together.

Did the Movement for Change develop you personally?

Yes, but this book is not a biography about me!

Some Movement for Change organisers said their campaign did move you personally?

That's very fair. Any election is emotional and it was very useful. It proved its worth with me and more widely.

The fall

There was no doubt that when David Miliband became the first candidate to enter the leadership race after Labour lost the election, he and his team were expecting to win. By the time September came around four months later, the odds seemed less certain, but the expectation was still running high. The signs were stamped all over the conference in Manchester. Most of the main hotels were booked out under David Miliband, leaving one of Ed Miliband's key campaigners to remark that he was "unable to find a room". Those who wanted to witness his predicted victory had made their bookings well in advance. Meanwhile some 200 conference tickets had been bought up by Lord Sainsbury for the Movement for Change campaigners so that members who might not normally have expected to come to conference could witness David Miliband's predicted inauguration. Even the timetable gave away the expectation that David Miliband would win. The result was expected to be announced at the beginning of the conference, but the Movement for Change assembly, where the full showcase of the campaign's achievements over the last four months was to be presented, was not going to be held until a few days later. There was no way the team expected to lose. The banners that were ordered to line the room had David Miliband's name on them.

The Movement for Change organisers had come down for their crowning moment. The fact that they still hadn't been fully accepted by David Miliband's campaign HQ was starkly apparent by the fact that they hadn't been booked hotels. Ten of them came down to stay in a two-bedroom flat, crashing on the floors whilst the rest of David Miliband's team enjoyed en suite bathrooms. As well as Stephens, Gabriel and Cox, there were a small group of other twenty-somethings attached to Citizens UK who wanted to be part of the final show, giving up their own money and time to be there for the big moment and perhaps a career break. Right up to the last minute David Miliband was expected to win, with influential bloggers predicting his victory less than a week before the result.

Glasman wasn't in Manchester the day the results came out. In fact he was in Shoreditch, standing at the altar of a wedding. He was the best man of William Taylor, the important friend and chaplain at London Metropolitan University who he had worked with on the City of London campaign. Glasman was standing next to Taylor at the altar listening to the wedding vows being announced, when he received a text message:

> I gently looked down and all I saw was two letters, that was "Ed"... I lifted my phone out of my pocket and there it was, then my phone went boom, boom, boom, and all the messages just said "Ed, Ed, Ed..."

> My instinctive first response was this massive feeling of joy! To be honest, I thought wow! This is going to be, my fear was David would win, my stuff would be seen as a community issue, and not central to the political economy and the policy that he would be surrounded by high level technocrats, and this would be a marginal part of the story. I just felt pleased for Ed, and excited... then I suddenly thought Oh my God, I thought of David, and the grief, and James, and the party, and the bitterness, and I thought, I'm glad I'm in Shoreditch today.

When the Citizens UK organisers found out, they were sitting at the back of a hall in Manchester. Once again they had been separated from the main campaign leaders and were squashed where they could find room. Cox, Gabriel and Stephens said they started the campaign fairly ambivalent about which leader they wanted to win. Their mission was simply to introduce community organising to the Labour party; it had just happened to be David Miliband that had given them the opportunity rather than his brother. But after all the energy and the work and the tension of the race – not to mention the earning of David Miliband's respect and their belief that they had touched him and earned his respect for their community movement – some kind of bond had developed. When the numbers came up, one organiser said they were "gutted".

It would have been impossible for David Miliband's team not to have raised questions of culpability here. Clearly some people blamed Movement for Change for taking up valuable resources when the result was so tight. However, Movement for Change organisers did not accept this. Later Cox said that they were just fulfilling their brief:

> the key thing was David's campaign never really wanted to do the full Obama community organising thing. They already had a plan to win the leadership election and the Movement for Change project was about how he was going to run the party after he had won. So at no point really was there any huge pressure on us to deliver the victory – so long as we weren't actively, you know, dissuading people from voting for him. We did do some stuff on recruiting people into membership and so on and so forth, but very limited. We could have done an

Obama-style thing where we invested a lot less in training and a lot more in mobilising but we were never asked to do that.

Glasman was more blunt. Reflecting on why David Miliband lost the leadership campaign that summer, he said it was because of his inability to fully commit to the Movement for Change. Although Glasman was perhaps not best placed to deliver lectures on commitment, he had his explanation straight:

> That failure to commit cost him [David Miliband] the job. It's what happens, he didn't seize it, he didn't make it his and he kept with a certain Blairism that ultimately was distrusted in too many sections of the party.

Just before David Miliband went home to let his brother have his moment, some forty people from his core campaign team gathered together in a restaurant in Manchester. Cox was in the room, and remembers being moved when David Miliband got up to speak:

> there was a very emotional dinner after we lost and David made this incredible speech and said whatever happens we have to continue Movement for Change – it's the most relevant thing we have done in this election, and, you know, it shouldn't be so associated with me that it now dies – it has to carry on and I have to find a way to make that happen. He could have blamed us and he didn't, we were a bit overwhelmed by that, there were people who came up and said; "We haven't always seen eye-to-eye throughout the campaign, but anything we can do to make this happen, you know, long term, we will

because we have seen it, and it needs to be tweaked, but we can see the value of it."

When the campaign came to a close, David Miliband remained understandably reluctant to give media interviews about why he lost. But one year on, the questions were put to him. The answers were not forthcoming:

Some interviewees suggested the fact you never fully decided what role M4C would play damaged your campaign?

You always wish that you have more time than you have, but I think we had a good balance. It was time well spent.

Would you do it differently if you had the chance?

I don't really go over that.

As for Glasman, he never publicly declared how he voted in the leadership election. When asked one year on, he said he still didn't want to say. All he wanted to add was that he "definitely ended with a stronger relationship with Ed". Throughout the course of the campaign it had become clear to Glasman that if Ed Miliband became leader, his ideas would have more influence over the party. David Miliband might have taken on the Movement for Change, but he had been unable to commit to it as much as Glasman would have liked and was unwilling to break from the Blairite model. Under David Miliband, Blue Labour ideas would be marginal. Under Ed Miliband, Glasman had a better chance of promoting Blue Labour.

Safe to say David Miliband's team never heard this perspective. Central members of his team – who remain good friends of Glasman – always thought he voted with them. When Cruddas found out about Glasman's expression of elation on Ed Miliband's victory almost a year later, he expressed a profound sense of surprise, asking five times whether Glasman had really reacted in that way. Glasman might have cared about relationships, but he also cared about results.

Pinning Ed

By their own admission, Citizens UK had made a "pittance" out of the David Miliband campaign. The hours they worked on the wage they were paid must have left them below the living wage they stood for. They had been continuously shut out of the mainstream David Miliband HQ. Now that David Miliband had lost, the sunk costs weren't going to pay back reputational dividends. But they weren't giving up. Still in the back of the room reeling after the result had been announced, Stephens remembers one point becoming clear to the organisers through the grief. They turned to each other and said, "We have to pin Ed."

The idea was simple. The assembly was still set up and ready to go. They had a room booked for 200 people, and 150 audience members had already been shipped down courtesy of Lord Sainsbury. It was only the distribution of power that had shifted. To make it work, they simply needed recognition from the new leader. Ed Miliband and his team would have to take the place of David Miliband, and make a public commitment to recognise the Movement for Change now that he was in office. Once this public declaration was made, Citizens UK could use this commitment as leverage over the leader during his time in post. They would be able to hold him accountable for keeping it going. It was the same strategy they played in the general election assembly with Brown and their August ceremony with David Miliband. Over the next three days on no wages, one of the organisers said they "worked like dogs" to make sure they were "buttonholing every Labour MP" that was at conference. It was a desperate attempt to try and save what they had built. Stephens remembers the heated negotiation:

> David knows the story, but Ed's team hasn't heard it. We didn't want all the hard work put into Movement to Change to end – there were so many people expecting it to be the foundations for real party change. We had seen what an appetite there was for relational organising. So, the day after the election results, we started negotiating, saying you need to come to our fringe event and you must ask Ed to come. This was when David's campaign showed just how much they cared about rebuilding the grassroots of the party because they were the ones facilitating those conversations and David's team backed us all the way, it was a really emotional time.

One particular introduction was key. Cox was introduced to Marcus Roberts, a field director from Ed Miliband's campaign. A consultant who had worked on Obama's election, Roberts was sympathetic towards the Movement for Change and their ideas. He went out on a limb to push for Ed Miliband to come to the assembly. It was difficult. This was a room of David Miliband supporters. It was unfamiliar, it was not part of the plan and it had every chance of back-firing. Roberts insisted that it would be fine, that it was courteous to recognise the other side and the work that they had done. Most importantly, he publicly assured Ed Miliband and his team that there would be "no surprises".

And he came. He was twenty minutes late, but Ed Miliband arrived into a room that was packed out. With extensive lobbying, the Citizens UK organisers had managed to get a number of significant players from Ed Miliband's campaign into the room with those who were directly involved with Movement for Change, and it was heaving. The testimony came on, the projects were celebrated, and Ed Miliband stepped on stage in the middle of it all. According to the organisers, his speech was warm and heartfelt. He told the audience that Movement for Change was the best part of David Miliband's campaign, and that he would continue to support it. The room cheered.

It was only when Ed Miliband finished speaking and was walking across the crowded room to leave, cameras flashing and people shouting, when the unexpected occurred. In usual style, Citizens UK had asked their members to chair the assembly. Heading up this particular session was Michael Beale, a trade unionist from Aylesbury who worked in Morrisons. Working on the minimum wage, he was married with two young children both with profound learning difficulties. He had been given a script to follow but Ed Miliband, who was not fully briefed, was walking out before it was over, surrounded by cameras and flashing lights. Beale's response was to tap loudly on the microphone:

Mr Miliband, Oh Mr Miliband, Mr Leader of the Labour Party... We're not finished yet.

It was a precious moment. Surrounded by everyone, Ed Miliband had to choose between walking away and looking like he was ignoring the grassroots he'd just committed to listening to, or staying and looking like he was under the thumb of a loon with a mike. Later, trade unionists would joke that it was the only time a union member had been able to pin the leader at party conference and hold them to account. Ed Miliband decided to stay. After Beale publicly informed the new leader that he had to win the next election for people like him who depended on it, Ed thanked him and left.

Once outside, Ed Miliband turned to Roberts, the man who had brought him into the room and said: "No surprises?"

But there were many more unexpected events to come. The first would occur less than a month later. David Miliband might have lost the leadership election, but he would continue to follow through with a set of seminars about the future of the Labour party with core members of his team. These meetings had been booked before the leadership election came to a close, and they were intended to continue the intellectual work that had started with the Movement for Change and develop a new policy platform for David Miliband's party. When Ed Miliband's team received invitations and went along to find David Miliband's team in the room with the older brother himself, the reaction couldn't have been anything other than complete shock.

Chapter Four

An Unexpected Guest

Most of the meetings that became known as the "Oxford Seminars" were held in the glamorous new-build extension to University College called the Butler Room.

Suspended above the master's private garden behind yellowing stonewalls and well-kept lawns, the extension is modelled on the grand surrounding architecture. Crowned with its own modern day turret, it sits back from the rest of the college, easily seen from the chapel's ancient stained glass windows. To reach it, you have to receive a nod from the porters keeping guard at the college's heavy oak doors. Then you have to cross through an expansive courtyard lined with elegant student rooms and white gilded window frames, or enter a locked gate from the college's high street entrance. Looking through the wrought iron bars at the Butler room floating above a secret garden dotted with purple and yellow flowers, there is something otherworldly about the place. An ivory tower, in the classic sense.

To get to the room itself you have to climb a dark wooden staircase. Pass through the elliptical wooden doors at the top, and you find yourself cupped in the Butler Room's white, curved walls. It feels more like an art gallery than a seminar room. You can smell the new pine floorboards and a faint undertone of gravy from past functions. A modern portrait of former US President Bill Clinton hangs on one wall, painted with contemporary bright colours and an exaggerated nose. The chairs are high quality plastic, and the tables on wheels easily slot together to form a large circle suitable for debate. When seated, the participants must have looked like the academic knights of the Ikea round table. Outside, the room's new windows look out on plush old English trees thick with emerald leaves, interrupted only by steeples and spires. The church bells of college chapels ring distantly through the glass.

Outside the college walls, the rest of Oxford is changing. The brightly coloured brands of high street banks – Santander, Natwest, Barclays – stamp reminders of the banking crisis around the central high street. Tesco Metro and Sainsburys Local nestle under the historic buildings with mossy roofs, selling produce to students strapped for cash and time. The autumn of 2010 when the Oxford seminars were being held, the air was thick with the politics of student funding. Massive protests were being held over the Coalition's tripling of tuition fees, and their actions were dominating the news bulletins and the university's central student union, OUSU. The country was angry, and the Coalition wasn't moving. Students were being kettled, arrests were being made and the windows at Conservative headquarters at Millbank, Westminster, were smashed in. Student occupations were going on in Oxford too, with some 70 students being evicted from the Bodleian Library around the corner from University

College on 25th November. One of the leading academics in the seminar, Stuart White, later lamented that most of the participants hadn't visited the occupations or thoroughly discussed the students' plight during meetings, particularly given their calls for the party to reconnect with grassroots movements.

The majority of the four seminars were held between October 2010 and April 2011 in this hothouse of the country's intellectual elite. Billed as a space to generate new ideas, the seminars brought together academics and top politicians less than four weeks after Ed Miliband had won the leadership battle. Although the work that emerged from them was attributed to Blue Labour, they were never advertised or organised with that intention. Indeed, some of the most high profile members in the room might well not have been in attendance if they were.

The seminars had an extraordinarily magnetic pull on both Milibands. David Miliband attended most of them even though he was widely believed to have stepped aside from mainstream Labour politics at the time. Senior political advisers of Ed Miliband's team also turned up eager to claim some of the terrain. The intellectual fallout of these meetings would go on to form what became known as the "Blue Labour Bible". The official title of this ebook – *The Labour Tradition and the Politics of Paradox* – might have been less glamorous, but that didn't stop it generating an explosion of publicity once it became known – albeit unfairly – as the definitive guide to Blue Labour philosophy. Everyone in the Butler Room knew that the ideas they were discussing were big and important themes for the Labour party, but very few could predict that their work would go viral. Jonathan Rutherford, the politically connected academic from Middlesex University and editor of the *Soundings Journal* who organised the meetings, had helped publish many ebooks in the past on different themes of the radical left, but none that would take off like this. The ebook resulting from these seminars would be downloaded over 100,000 times in the first five weeks of its publication, and would be quoted again and again by the mainstream press, with many of its lines – often used off hand – coming back to haunt the individuals involved. It was beyond the wildest expectations of any of the attendants that this was what they were creating. They could not imagine that the ideas they were discussing would eventually generate as much media attention as anything else the rest of the party would come up with, catching the leader's eye.

The founding four

There were four key academics involved in leading and organising the seminars. Rutherford was the "engine room" of the seminars – collating contributions, liaising with publishers and setting up a Google mailing group for participants to continue discussions outside of the room. Professor of cultural studies at Middlesex, Rutherford had written extensively about issues of identity and morality under capitalism, including a number of articles for the *New Statesman* and the *Guardian*. Tall, slim with silver hair, Rutherford had a calm way of expressing an ever anxious set of concerns. Later, he was to become one of the most worried about the Blue Labour brand. Rutherford was also a longstanding friend of Jon Cruddas, the MP for the constituency now known as

Dagenham and Rainham, who ran for deputy leader against Harriet Harman. Cruddas was Rutherford's chief link to the political world, who remained highly committed to the seminars and encouraged his political and academic contacts to attend. It was Cruddas who had first urged Rutherford to meet Glasman, and the pair had formed a friendship, with Rutherford regularly coming over to Glasman's flat on Friday nights.

The second was Marc Stears, the politics tutor at University College where the seminars were hosted. Raised in South Wales, this rather neat man in glasses went on to study at Oxford at the same time as Ed Miliband before becoming a politics tutor there himself. Stears specialised in political theory, radicalism and political protest, and had a keen interest in American politics. In 2011, he became a visiting fellow at the lef-wing think tank IPPR, conducting a research project on left of centre parties in the UK. He met a key political contact for the seminars – former work and pensions secretary James Purnell – through the country's other major left of centre think tank, Demos. On leaving office, Purnell launched a three-year study at the organisation in 2009 to explore what it meant to be on the left and encourage pluralism. These meetings made many of the significant introductions that underpinned the relationships in the seminars. The third academic leading the meetings was Stuart White, a political theory tutor at Jesus College who also had independent links with Cruddas through various conferences and contributions to left wing blogs. Less politically invested in the Labour party, White was a measured, softly spoken contributor who was interested in wider debates about social justice, liberty and equality, getting involved with the local anti-cuts movement in Oxford. The fourth academic was Glasman.

From David to Ed

Looking back on the seminars, the key organisers insist that they were not trying to lay the intellectual groundwork for Blue Labour. Marc Stears says it is "important to stress there was no agenda… it wasn't as if we were launching a program". At most it was an informal space for some important players to explore shared ideas and common ground in the context of Labour's election defeat and a change of leadership. There was no formal policy-making process in play, let alone any official declaration of a new Blue Labour camp. In fact when discussing one of the final contributions to the resulting ebook, Rutherford explicitly asked White not to include the phrase Blue Labour, but to refer simply to "radical conservatism". The final ebook was only attributed to Blue Labour after it exploded onto the media scene some months later. At the time Blue Labour was not a nationally recognised brand; it was a quirky turn of phrase from a professor most people hadn't heard of. Glasman might have mentioned it, but when the first meeting was held, he was not a Lord or labelled as "Ed's guru" throughout the media. He was just another academic in the room.

So what was the real motivation for the seminars? According to one member of Ed Miliband's team, these meetings had originally been designed to be an interesting space for David Miliband to develop his policy agenda after he had won the leadership battle. He might have lost, but the seminars were still booked. Certainly looking at the political representation in the room, the seminars were connected with David Miliband's people. David Miliband attended most of the sessions personally, and with him came other political figures who were explicitly in his camp throughout the summer. James Purnell was there. Cruddas was also a strong supporter of David Miliband whilst being very close to Jonathan Rutherford. The only other elected political representatives in the room – David Lammy, Tessa Jowell, Hazel Blears – had all preferred David Miliband over his younger brother. This is perhaps not surprising, given that the idea for the seminars was developed during a Trade Union Congress workshop in May 2010, where David Miliband spoke alongside Cruddas after the former had announced his intention to run for leader.

Strategic motivations aside, it would be a mistake to assume that the Oxford Seminars weren't a genuine attempt to find new intellectual ground. Several of the leading academics were Ed Miliband supporters, and others were ambivalent about sibling rivalry. Many had come together out of a simple frustration with the status quo. Labour had pulled the country back from the brink of financial crisis, but it was hard for the party not to accept some culpability for both failing to take action earlier. The participants genuinely wanted to review the facts and change the party. The financial crisis had struck a heavy blow to New Labour's political economy, and something had to change. Even with extra spending, after three terms in government, the gap between rich and poor was wider than when Tony Blair took office, and the economy was less diverse. Labour had got a new leader, but it still lacked fresh ideas. By Ed Miliband's own admission, he didn't have all the answers, and the party was still in shock at his surprise ascendency to leader. New direction was essential. It would be wrong to say that the seminars were not a genuine attempt to find it.

With the leadership lost and Ed Miliband's team in the room, it is hard to find an ulterior motive that would bring a demoralised David Miliband into the room, besides a genuine commitment to exploring the ideas discussed and perhaps a hope that he might still at some stage succeed his younger brother. At the time, his presence defied the image of the near Labour leader. In the autumn the press portrayed him as slinking into the shadows after defeat, avoiding all engagement on domestic political matters. Now here he was engaging with a policy group that had been planned for him at the very beginning of his leadership campaign. His political supporters had still come out for him, and he continued to contribute to the discussion and return when he saw senior members of Ed Miliband's team in the room. He might have left the Labour party conference early, but he certainly wasn't leaving the policy debate.

Although the seminars had been planned for a while, Ed Miliband's political advisers said they received an invitation only after Ed Miliband's victory. The fact that they didn't make any formal submission to the ebook other than a last-minute foreword suggests that they were there to monitor rather than contribute to the discussion. Indeed at the first seminar, there was no one from Ed Miliband's office in attendance – they said they were simply "too busy to attend". But at the second seminar Ed Miliband's policy officer Greg Beales arrived and, significantly, the third meeting was attended by the leader's strategy adviser Stewart Wood.

For all the David Miliband supporters in the room, it was obvious that the balance of power in the seminars was now very different to what participants had originally intended. Even Rutherford, who insisted that the seminars were never just about David Miliband, admitted that the leadership outcome "wasn't as people expected". Although the older brother's contributions held weight and gravitas, they did not exert overwhelming influence. David Miliband was not sitting at the top of the Labour party as many participants had hoped, even if he did still get mobbed by students wanting to talk to him on the way to Oxford station. For the seminars to have bite, they would have to look to other players in the room. Those, in short, who were more connected to his younger brother.

From David Miliband's perspective this must have seemed odd. He was sitting in the seminars that had been designed to kickstart his leadership and develop trains of thought set in play by the Movement for Change campaign, but suddenly there were flies on the wall. Everyone in the room knew it, and no one could do anything about it. David Miliband and his team were left in a position where either their seminars were not going to have any influence, or they would be picked up and used, but only to serve the administration of his brother. Even the most high minded individual wishing to put new ideas for the party over sibling rivalry must have found the dynamic difficult to ignore just weeks after his leadership defeat.

So how did the gulf between the two brothers get bridged? There weren't many participants at the seminars who had remained on good working terms with both brothers during the leadership campaign. Glasman had of course tried, but that had proven to be a source of further division rather than unity. But there was one institution that crossed the boundaries between David Miliband and Ed Miliband: Oxbridge. It didn't matter if you were in the Ed or David Miliband camp, because both camps were pitched well within the elite institutions' grounds, and this provided scope for a good deal of overlap.

Take Marc Stears. He knew James Purnell from the Demos Open Left series, which gave him an introduction to David Miliband's team. But he also knew Ed Miliband from his time at Oxford, as they had both studied at Corpus Christi together. Stears had been an avid fan of Ed Miliband since university, describing him as a "coalition builder", a student who could talk to anyone from the top private schools to the poorest comprehensives and find common ground. Stuart White was a friend and colleague of Stears, but had also got to know Cruddas through shared conferences and the blogosphere. Rutherford and Glasman were amongst the few key players in the room who were not Oxbridge graduates.

These links also extended to Citizens UK. Stefan Baskerville, a young Oxford graduate who was heavily involved in Citizens UK and helped out on David Miliband's campaign, also attended the seminars. Glasman had credited Baskerville, a student of Stears, for his introduction to the tutor after Baskerville interviewed him for his thesis on community organising. It was Baskerville who also first introduced Sophie Stephens, another Oxford graduate, to Citizens UK just a few years before.

The linchpin

But it was one particular Oxbridge man that was responsible for bridging the gap between Ed Miliband and the heavy predominance of David Miliband fans at the seminars; the academic and strategy adviser Stewart Wood. He had met Ed Miliband in Berlin at a research institute. Ed Miliband was visiting whilst studying at the LSE at the time, whilst Wood was a PhD student at Harvard. Ed Miliband had helped him get a job with Gordon Brown, who he served for ten years before helping Ed Miliband with his leadership campaign. Now Wood had been rewarded with a peerage and the title of strategy adviser to the new Labour leader. Appointed as shadow member without portfolio, he had significant clout at the top of the party. But as an Oxford tutor who continued to work at the university, he was also very close to the academics involved in leading the seminars. Crucially, he worked in the same department as Stears and the pair had overlapped as students at the same university. Wood had also collaborated with White, co-editing a book together in 1996 and contributing to another publication White had written on the future of New Labour in 2001. He clearly had an attachment and deep sympathy to the ideas being discussed, lecturing on British politics with a keen interest in political economy. Close to Ed Miliband and the academics involved in the seminars, Wood would prove to be the crucial linchpin for Glasman's ascendance to the Lords, and the resulting rise in profile of the seminars' ebook. It was Wood that would eventually seal Ed Miliband's stamp of approval on the seminars, penning the foreword to the ebook on behalf of the party leader just a few minutes before publication.

Wood's first appearance was at the third seminar, held in Oxford. Although the large presence of David Miliband supporters in the room did lead him to raise an eyebrow, his personal connections with the academics and ideas involved meant he didn't approach the meetings with a sense of threat or hostility. It is likely that he would have approached the meeting differently if he felt uncomfortable behind the prestigious university's walls. But Wood was on home ground, and clearly shared an interest in many of the ideas being discussed. As he put it:

> Many of the people who attended the seminars were at the time more naturally David supporters than Ed supporters in the campaign, but Ed had a strong interest in many of the core ideas – such as a different approach to the financial services sector, making the Labour party a genuine community movement, and talking about the limits of markets in our towns and cities.

It would have been easy to dismiss these seminars and their ideas as the last remnants of the David Miliband's team, or to treat them as toxic by association with the Blairite camp. But in fact Wood showed respect for the ideas at play, and for the subtlety of David Miliband's position. He understood why the ideas appealed to David Miliband, and why they could still be useful to the party. Most importantly, Wood was personally interested in the ideas being discussed. He had met Glasman during the leadership campaign after Glasman's name "kept coming up". They had talked at length in Glasman's notorious Soho coffee bar hang out to discuss ideas, and found a number of shared interests, particularly on German political economy and workers representation. Clearly there was some sense that the ideas being discussed in Oxford were not just for David Miliband, but could well be consistent and useful for Ed Miliband's project.

Core participants at the Oxford seminars:

Stefan Baskerville	David Miliband
Hazel Blears	Duncan O'Leary
Phillip Collins	Anthony Painter
Graeme Cooke	James Purnell
Jon Cruddas	Jonathan Rutherford
Sally Davison	Marc Stears
Maurice Glasman	Jon Stokes
Ben Jackson	Andrea Westall
Mike Kenny	Stuart White
David Lammy	Jon Wilson

This list is limited to key players. There may have been some variation between sessions. Greg Beales, Stewart Wood and Tessa Jowell were also in regular attendance but didn't contribute to the final ebook.

As might be expected from "Camp David", the Blairite wing of the party was heavily represented at the seminars, with individuals like Phil Collins championing Blairite values and ideas. But it would be a mistake to think that the meetings represented a homogenous political faction. Sally Davison, the managing editor of *Soundings* for example, was there representing the Gramscian

Eurocommunist left of the 1970s. Stuart White held a more democratic socialist position. Cruddas was another participant who frequently defied labels from the left and right, but somehow managed to commandeer the respect of both. The only groups that seemed to be obviously underrepresented were the Fabians and the Brownites. This was a symbolic omission given the seminars' critique of the state, but certainly in the case of the Fabians it was not deliberate. Sunder Katwala, the chair of the traditionally more pro-state wing of the party, had been invited but was simply unable to make it. The participants represented a genuinely diverse group, brought together out of frustration with the status quo. A coalition, some might say, of disaffection. Of course, the fact that it was diverse does not mean that it was accessible. Others allegedly mentioned to Glasman that they wanted to come to this rather prestigious meeting, but the Butler Room was deemed to be full. As Rutherford put it:

> We never said anyone couldn't come. That isn't to say that lots of people wouldn't have liked to have come, but we didn't publicise it. We were operating under Chatham House, but there was a sense that it shouldn't be talked about in media or print. A few journalists wanted to mention the seminars and we said don't. It would be unhelpful.

The seminars themselves always followed the same pattern. The participants would meet between 2pm – 4pm on Monday afternoons. The four key academics in the room – Glasman, Stears, Rutherford and White – would take it in turns to present a paper that they had written and circulated a week before the seminar. A short summary of the paper would then be presented by the writer at the beginning of each session for about ten minutes. Another academic in the key group of four would then give a formal response, before questions and comments were opened up to the floor. Each month the four would rotate, taking it in turns to present, chair and respond at each session.

Seminar 1 Monday 18th October, "Labour as a radical tradition" Maurice Glasman, respondent Marc Stears, University College, Oxford.

Seminar 2 Monday 29th November "Leadership, Democracy, and Organising". Marc Stears, respondent Jonathan Rutherford, London Metropolitan University.

Seminar 3 Monday 24th January "The future is conservative", Jonathan Rutherford, respondent Stuart White, University College, Oxford.

Seminar 4 Monday 21st March Oxford, four responses on the papers and series in general from Stuart White, Tessa Jowell, Hazel Blears, Jon Cruddas, University College, Oxford.

According to White, the atmosphere in the seminars was "business-like". There was no Citizens UK style introduction to the players in this room; no intimate one to ones or personal revelations about their deepest motivations for getting into politics or ideals for the country. Most of the relationships in this seminar had already been forged in the fire of government or the heat of academic term time. The big political figures were clearly recognised from TV; it was not felt necessary to give further introduction. David Miliband took his seat, Ed Miliband sent his regards to Glasman via text, and the meeting began.

Glasman was to present the first paper of the first session. Later this would become the first chapter of the ebook. He had publicly denounced the dominance of the university's PPE graduates amongst the political class, now he was meeting at their source. He shuffled into his seat looking scruffier than the rest and started his presentation.

The paper was a call for the Labour party to return to what Glasman saw as its traditional roots in the Labour movement. It laid out a history of the party as he saw it, accusing New Labour of over-emphasising 1945 and sidelining its gritty history of worker participation and grassroots movements. Under the heading "Meet the Family" Glasman traced Labour's values back to Aristotle and the notion of a common good politics. He threaded that Aristotelian link through the Tudor commonwealth tradition, GDH Cole and Tawney. Glasman then laid out what he called the second thread of Labour history; a narrative path through the Norman conquest and the rights of the Englishman, and the people's fight for their rights to the land. He linked labour history right through from the Dockers Strike of 1889 to Citizens UK's campaign for a living wage today. He criticised New Labour's light touch with the market and heavy handedness with the state, and sought to place the party back in the community. He attacked all this and more, right in the faces of many of those politicians who had been responsible for that same order in the room.

The alternative, argued Glasman, was to get back to Labour's roots, when there was emotion in Labour politics and reciprocity in the state's relationships:

> Labour values are not abstract universal values such as "freedom" or "equality". Distinctive labour values are rooted in relationships, in practices that strengthen an ethical life. Practices like reciprocity, which gives substantive form to freedom and equality in an active relationship of give and take. Mutuality, where we share the benefits and burdens of association. And then if trust is established, solidarity, where we actively share our fate with other people.

Glasman argued that all the answers to reforming Labour's current politics, which appeared soulless and hollowed out, could be addressed by relearning neglected aspects of its own tradition. The crucial, radical part of this history, argued Glasman, was resisting the unrestrained domination of capitalism through relationships:

> It is a radical tradition that is as committed to the preservation of meaning and status as it is to democratic egalitarian change, and seeks to pursue both. This gives tremendous resources and possibilities to the Labour tradition as it seeks to renew its sense of political relevance in political circumstances that threaten its rationality and purpose. This requires, and has always required, an organised resistance to the logic of finance capitalism, and a strengthening of democratic institutions of self-government.

Stears was officially charged with responding to the paper. Although wishing to respect the Chatham House rules of the seminar, Stears said it was "very well received". Purnell later said he "loved it". Here was something different and interesting. In particular, Glasman's ideas were radical but they did not advocate a massive increase in state spending. Blairite ears pricked up at that. It was also one of the few narratives that seemed to respond to the Big Society rhetoric of the Tory administration, without looking like Labour was following their opponents' lead. It is just a shame, Stears says, that some of the nuances of Glasman's paper have been lost since the seminars:

> It was very much in the view of the seminar the idea that there were two strands of Labour thinking a kind of managerial strand a more democratic strand, a state strand and a local strand and they always existed in combination of each other and the party was at its best when the combination was at its most intense and at its worst when one strand was more dominant over another that was how the conversation went and I think it's sad that's been overlooked in the debate since which has tended to be position as though one strand is better than another and that's not how it was received at the time. Localism, democratic engagement, relationship building they all matter and we have overlooked them but it's not like they are the only things that matter.

Despite the tension that would follow the publication of the ebook and the unusual composition of the room, Stears says the atmosphere at the time was wholly positive:

> I thought it [the atmosphere in the seminars] was terrific, it was you know the first one was somewhat, there was some nervousness as David was going to be there and I hadn't seen him

since the leadership result and no one knew what that would mean but right from the start here was a positive atmosphere … I think that we all thought it went better than we imagined it might, partly as there was such a buy-in from politicians across the spectrum and that was what we hoped it would be, it was neither an academic nor a factional discussion, it was an open argument across different parts of the party and that was a nice moment.

Rutherford agreed:

We came from the outside coming in, so we weren't immersed in that rivalry or all the tensions of the leadership campaign. It is overplayed. As far as the organising of the seminars and the atmosphere and what was picked up we didn't pick up the tension. It was very good discussions felt very engaged and lots of energy and that came out in what people wrote afterwards. People were just willing to write 5,000 words quickly.

The surprise

The first seminar then, was regarded as a success. The tension of the leadership campaign had been bracketed in the name of new ideas, and the discussions had proven by all accounts to be interesting and insightful. Some kind of equilibrium had been established.

But between the first and second seminar, a major change happened that shifted the balance of power once again. Glasman received a phone call from Stewart Wood telling him he was going to be made a lord. This single, brief call altered everything. Glasman, who had entered as a rogue academic that it was difficult to take seriously, was now receiving a peerage, and this elevated him above his academic peers. The remarks Glasman had made in the first seminar had gone from the ramblings of one man to a contribution from a high-profile political figure, personally appointed by the party leader, who would now sit alongside Lord Wood as a colleague. It was a further sign of Ed Miliband's invisible but tangible presence in the room. The news came as a shock to everyone, not least to the future lord himself, who later said the surprise phone call had left him "completely flabbergasted".

The real question buzzing in the heads of all those in the seminar, was *Why Glasman?* What was the motivation behind this unexpected elevation? One member of the seminars – who preferred not to be named – suspected it was about "owning" Glasman, a defiant sign to his brother that this man and his ideas were now his territory. But members of Ed Miliband's office insisted that it had nothing to do with David Miliband, or feeling threatened by the seminars. Members of the leader's office had after all been invited to the meetings, and the election was complete. According to Wood, the real motivation was surprisingly simple and genuine. Ed Miliband wanted to recognise Glasman and – to a certain extent – his Blue Labour ideas. In a commitment to openness and debate that contrasted with some aspects of past Labour leaders, Ed Miliband later said he was deliberately giving Glasman a platform to make sure that his avant-garde voice was heard. He added that Glasman did some "useful space creating" for the party, providing an opportunity for new "ideas to flourish".

The second seminar then, had a very different tone. Glasman had told key players in the seminars – Rutherford, Purnell and Cruddas – about his offer and they all congratulated him and encouraged him to accept it. Although none said they recognised Glasman's appointment as having any direct implications for their work at the time, it would change the place of the seminars in Labour history. In that next meeting though, it felt more of a personal issue.

The second seminar was held on Glasman's home turf at London Metropolitan University, hosted by the new future peer. It was also the day of a London tube strike and an intense snowstorm, so it was difficult to organise. Stears was presenting, and many participants came in late and slightly ruffled from the journey. Stears' paper was about the need for the Labour party to become a better, renenergised campaigning organisation. He argued that the party should be about more than trying to get out the vote during elections, but should actually seek to become part of a social movement. Arguing along the lines of Saul Alinsky, Stears made the case for the power of relationships, stating that action should be grounded in a thorough understanding of power rather than faith in idealism alone. Labour's fundamental task, he concluded, involved enabling people to create their own change in their own neighbourhoods, giving them a sense of power and ownership:

> It is when people come together locally to save a library, help set up a new day care centre, or clean up decaying public spaces, that they begin to feel bonds of solidarity with each other that do not currently exist. This is a powerful basis for Labour renewal.

Although a close friend of Ed Miliband, Stears acknowledged that David Miliband's Movement for Change campaign was the closest Labour had come to implementing his ideas. But despite the tension of the recent leadership campaign, there seemed to be little hard feeling. No allegation was made about the stealing of ideas, and full credit was given where it was due. Stears explicitly praised the Movement For Change organiser, Sophie Stephens, for her work over the summer.

The third seminar was held back in Oxford, and Jonathan Rutherford was presenting. His paper argued that Labour was at risk of losing the support of working people who gave the party life, and called for a return to a political order that was about "community work, country and a sense of honour". He painted a picture of Britons living in an anxious age that politicians have been unable to respond to. He said that Labour needed to rediscover a language that spoke to people's concerns, and addressed their desire for stability:

> Labour's future is conservative. It needs to rediscover England's radical traditions that are rooted in the long political struggle against dispossession. This includes reconnecting with an English socialism that grew out of the struggles for land and for the ownership of one's own labour against the forces of the market and of arbitrary power.

According to players in the room, there was quite a critical response to this presentation. There was a general concern that the ideas being presented were nostalgic, although the room was divided about whether or not it would be possible to work around that objection. David Miliband was particularly outspoken. One participant remembered him saying that although there might be some parts of the conservative tradition worth returning to, he was wary of making Labour's central message a call to "stop changing things". Some months later David Miliband said that he took a lot from the seminars, particularly the "founding insight" that "significant relationships can counter the power of the market and the state", but he agreed that this needed to be achieved in a modern context:

> We discussed the danger of nostalgia which is real. We need forward looking relationships not backward looking ones, there was a real consensus around that point in the discussions … And of course the devil is in practical application in policies and practices that make a difference.

In the final seminar held on March 21st 2011, the context had changed dramatically again. Since Glasman's appointment to the Lords had been publicly announced in November, Blue Labour had begun to snowball in the press. Glasman had given an interview for the *Times* where he criticised David Miliband for being "non-relational" and the *Observer* did a profile on him in January. Meanwhile one of the seminars had been cancelled for organisational reasons, and the participants hadn't met for two months. Perhaps it is not surprising then that White suggested that instead of introducing a new theme, he would use his presentation to give a round-up of the three papers presented so far. In any case, he believed introducing his research interests on wider social movements would seem disjointed.

In the final paper of the seminars, White argued that there really was a coherent narrative linking the three preceding presentations. The work of Stears, Glasman and Rutherford, he believed, hung together as a coherent whole. They were addressing more than three subjects on the same theme; together they constituted a substantial body that – if not at all polished or complete – laid some solid foundations for a theory that had a "distinctive view about what Labour politics is and should be". In particular, White argued that this "Radical Conservatism" had five key strands, which he later published as the core points of Blue Labour on the blog Open Democracy:

1   A politics of conservation. Radical politics ought to be centrally about the protection of identities and sources of personal meaning based on place and/or work. In particular, radical politics is about protecting them against erosion by mobile capital.

2   A politics of participatory democracy. Radical politics should look to popular self-organization to defend the integrity of these identities and sources of meaning. This (according to Blue Labour) has always been what the labour movement, at its best, is about. Today, this tradition of self-organisation to restrain capital finds expression in community organising of the kind practised by Citizens UK.

3   A politics of ownership. Radical politics must take the ownership of property seriously. The power of capital within the firm should not be that of an unaccountable sovereign, but a power that is balanced by workers' rights. Capital should not be entirely footloose, but entangled and grounded within specific places, e.g., by vesting local civil society with the ownership of productive assets.

4 Less moral abstraction. Radical politics should not base its claims in "abstract" notions like fairness, equality, social justice or rights which are remote from people's life experiences and immediate concerns. It should base itself on concrete grievances and historical traditions that are part of people's identity.

5 Less emphasis on state welfare. Radical politics should give less emphasis than social democracy conventionally does to redistribution, welfare transfers and the state as a financer and provider of services.

Of course, having a coherent narrative does not necessarily mean that everyone agrees it is the right one to pursue. White acknowledged later that there were very different reactions when it came to judging the value of the ideas proposed. In fact he said there were broadly four positions that emerged in the room:

On the one hand there were some people who thought Blue Labour an attractive, coherent perspective and who were generally favourable to it – I think Jon Wilson was very sympathetic to the perspective. Then there was a perspective in the room that this is on to something but we need to combine it with the best of New Labour – the Blue and the New – that comes out of some of the contributions – Graeme Cook wrote on those lines. Then there were people like me who were engaging with it from a sort of traditional social democratic perspective and what could we learn from Blue Labour to renew and renovate a social democracy committed to economic egalitarianism. That was perhaps less prominent in the discussions. Sally Davison might have had a similar perspective. There were also people who identified with a tradition of libertarian socialism harking back to guild socialism and the co-operative movement and who were engaging with this as a way of trying to rejuvenate Labour around these things. I think Andrea Westall is very much in this co-operative tradition. These categories aren't mutually exclusive. My sense is that Tessa Jowell was sympathetic to the "Blue and the New" perspective but she is also interested in that cooperative tradition. These categories overlap.

Later some bitterness emerged about the three papers being lumped together. The writers had only ever been interested in developing shared themes, and it was intriguing that White had found some coherent overlap, but the media would end up binding the writings together in a philosophy that the participants had never officially signed up for. What White had meant to identify as interesting points of consensus was later mistaken for being a united, deliberate Blue Labour programme. Others in the room were less convinced about the coherence. They would became less convinced as time went on and the profile of Glasman continued to rise. When asked in July 2011 whether he believed there was ever a coherence to the papers, Stears admitted that there was a shared understanding between the contributors that the Blair/Brown model was broken, but there were important points of difference on what exactly should take its place:

there were certainly common themes, but there are also significant differences between the three major papers and I worry
that the resulting debate overlooked those crucial differences
and as a result I mean people attributed things that Jonathan
Rutherford wrote to Maurice for example and I think that is
bizarre, if you read the papers they are very different, there are
important points of connection but there are important differences of style and argument as well and I'm not sure if those
differences came out in the subsequent debate but it certainly
came out in the debate of the seminars.

When the seminars first concluded though, none of this
divergence seemed to matter. When the meetings came to an
end, they did so without event, celebration or media interest.
There was no sense that the participants had produced a
ground-breaking body of work that would lay the foundations for significant media interest, let alone a political
programme. In fact it was quite the opposite. By themselves,
the Oxford seminars seemed abstract and disconnected from
the mainstream political process. They might have raised big
and important questions, but they were expected to have
little influence over policy because they were not tied to the
leadership or the party's mainstream power base in any meaningful way. Worse, they were tied to a defunct power base, a
man who never won. Ed Miliband's team were in the room,
but they had been peripheral to the process. Little wonder
then, that the seminars received little attention. Most Labour
politicians in the parliamentary party – including the deputy
leader Harriet Harman – knew almost nothing about them.
It was widely understood that the original plan was to hold
six seminars, not four. Although none of the participants

wanted to go on the record with their comments, the general consensus from those involved was that the seminars seemed to "fizzle out".

It is somewhat suprising then that the work from the seminars went on to gain such a high profile. When the ebook was eventually published in May, it received 22,000 downloads in the first ten hours, and over 100,000 hits by June. The real explanation behind this suprise boom in interest was Glasman's ascension to the Lords.

Through his acceptance of Ed Miliband's offer, Glasman was catapulted into the political spotlight, stimulating a new and growing interest in his work. He had been endorsed by the leader, and his eccentric character was pounced on by the media. He had the ear of the leader, but more importantly than that, he *appeared* to have the ear of the leader. That meant that when Glasman went on to talk about the Blue Labour ideas he had begun discussing in the ebook, they were linked to Ed Miliband, and thereby linked to the public's vision of the new post Blair-Brown Labour party. Out of government, perception is all the power the Labour leader had. Now he was sharing it with Glasman.

If Glasman's opening contribution to *The Labour Tradition* raised the profile of the ebook, Wood's interest in the seminars and his last-minute foreword – penned on behalf of the Labour leader – was the crowning touch. Between them, Wood and Glasman stamped Ed Miliband's approval on a set of policies that were originally designed to enrich his brother's leadership.

The ideas from the ebook would go on to have an influence over policy, albeit through the indirect route of Glasman and his new media soapbox. New policy angles, lines from speeches and proposals to reform and open up the party's structures, would later be traced back and credited to Glasman's influence. The Oxford Seminars may have initially been convened for David Miliband's team, but now they had been absorbed into Ed Miliband's agenda. They had found a route to power once again.

Chapter Five

A Test of Friendship

The terrace at the House of Lords juts out over the river Thames like a ship. As a newly-made peer, it was Glasman's new favourite space. Out in the open air, it allowed him to smoke freely. His own self-designated table sat closest to the water. It became littered with his signature possessions: a blue and orange packet of Old Holborn tobacco, a lighter, a pair of glasses, empty coffee cups and his pair of mobile phones. Across the river, St Thomas' hospital looms up behind the green tree-lined streets of the Embankment. Boats of all kinds bob along the water. The great house's large sandy-coloured spires stretch high overhead. The sound of Big Ben chiming next door echoes warmly across the roof as smartly dressed waiters hand out cream cakes and neat sandwiches. From the very beginning of his peerage Glasman had made a conscious effort to get to know the Lords' staff, proudly calling them by their first names in front of visitors. They smile and nod at him as he twitchily rolls up, sips his coffee, and strides around the terrace. Glasman's friends and visitors used to come to Bar Italia in Soho to sit outside and talk to the little-known academic while he smoked. Now Lord Glasman would see his visitors here.

Glasman might have had an unconventional background for a Lord, but anyone who went to visit him in Westminster acknowledged that he was now in his element. His love of tradition and heritage gave Glasman a huge appreciation for the building. He would enthusiastically take his guests around the chambers, pointing out the virtuous stories of King Arthur and the knights of the round table depicted on the walls and stopping to stare wide eyed every time he passed the House's copy of the Magna Carta. Of course he still made mistakes. One of his first public introductions to the Lords was walking into the chamber the wrong way. Mistakenly crossing in front of the speaker, he caused the whole house to shout for order. Outside of the chamber, many on the left criticised Glasman for taking up a position that was not democratically elected, but the criticisms held little weight with the academic. In his eyes the Lords was a place of virtue and tradition, perfectly suited to his Blue Labour philosophy. The left's connection with what he perceived to be an abstract, liberal sense of fairness – almost always articulate by middle class critics – left him cold. He had an emotional connection with the place. His mum, after all, would have been proud.

Looking back on the call when Stewart Wood first told him about the honour, Glasman's surprise and delight is still palpable:

> First of all I had no idea really what it meant, it never crossed my mind, such a thing, it was genuinely outside my experience. I didn't know what Lords did and what that would mean. I

remember saying something really stupid like "You have to give me a few days to talk to my people" and Stewart saying "You have 45 minutes, we only had the idea last night and the closure date is today at 5.30pm", so I think it was a last minute thought. I rang my wife who thought I was joking and it was one of those conversations and I said "Look I've got to give an answer" and she said "what are you serious?" and I said yes, and that was a really lovely laughter – everyone I told, their first response was a real laughter – a really long, strong genuine laugh. I rang Jon [Cruddas] and I rang James [Purnell] and they both said definitely and then began a whole new, I didn't realise what a big deal it would be, obviously I had to keep it quiet and then it was publicly announced, there was a lot of recognition for London Citizens, and for Blue Labour, this was a real, well, this was just a conversation that was going between people I was meeting, to reiterate there was no sense of building a movement, it was just an idea that was making friends. This made it more serious.

On a very practical level, Glasman's ascension to the Lords transformed his daily life by providing him with a new source of income. For some time the family's financial situation had been deteriorating. Three weeks before he was offered a place in the Lords, Glasman's wife Catherine applied for a job at Morrisons to make ends meet, and never got a reply. It got to the point, Glasman said, where it was getting difficult to meet costs for food. By taking up the peerage, he would receive £300 just for sitting in the chamber. It was literally an offer he couldn't refuse:

we had no money and we had another child, so we had four children in one bedroom, we had to borrow money, and there were some months we had none, and I kept saying we can't be dominated by money… cheques bouncing, and no food, when you have got four children the no food issue is tricky, we were living off carrots, the coffee and cigarette diet is quite longstanding at home.

The financial reward was transformational for Glasman. Overnight, his cash flow problems were over. He was able to take his family on their first proper holiday. More than that, his ten-year-old daughter Annie could now have her own separate room instead of sharing with her three brothers. With the new money that was coming in – combined with a new teaching grant he'd received – Glasman was now able to build an entire new level on his flat in Hackney. For his wife Catherine, who had worked her whole life to support others, it was a huge recognition to be made a Lady. Glasman said she had been a massive supporter of the Blue Labour project from the beginning, supporting her husband's community organising when it took up precious time without bringing in much-needed income. The whole family, Glasman said, felt "honoured" by Ed Miliband's decision.

The political consequences were also transformational. This was a big political gesture from Ed Miliband. The Labour leader was now offering public recognition to Glasman, formally endorsing his relationship with the rather unpredictable academic. This of course had significant consequences for Blue Labour. Glasman came with a brand, which meant Blue Labour now had a publicly recognised platform. By elevating Glasman to the Lords, Ed Miliband was giving credibility to a whole new set of ideas and values that he embodied. The fact that Ed Miliband was seen to have chosen Glasman was also very important to the media. From now on, when Glasman said something, it would be linked directly to the head of the party, and he was often referred to as "Ed's policy adviser" or "political guru". At a time when journalists were anxious to define the new – and slightly unexpected – leader of the opposition, Glasman provided a rather intriguing and colourful set of clues.

The transition was a fast one. Within the space of a few months, Glasman went from being an academic who could say what he pleased to an ennobled politician. From now on he would be judged very differently by the press and the public, and he would have to learn the hard way that this could have destructive as well as useful consequences. This was the period when Glasman began capturing the front pages of major national newspapers, but not as planned. Less than six months into his appointment, his media outbursts would earn him a reputation for controversy and put real strain on some of the most important relationships in Blue Labour. By the time parliament broke up for the summer, some of Glasman's closest alliances were at breaking point and he would have a personal warning from Ed Miliband. It would take Glasman time to calibrate his public commitments with his personal views, particularly when he was attached to attention and the idea that controversy could be a useful stimulus for debate. But now he was Lord the stakes were higher, as was the fall-out.

Brand Management

Although Glasman has often been portrayed as a one-man band – an individual eccentric who perhaps made more noise than his influence allowed – there were a number of other significant players that worked with him behind the scenes on the Blue Labour project. Many of these alliances were left over from the Oxford seminars. This group – which included the likes of Jon Cruddas and Marc Stears – had a stake in the ideas Glasman was promoting and therefore in his new-found influence in parliament. Although the seminars were never intended to produce a Blue Labour agenda, there was still sufficient overlap in the theories and ideas discussed in the Butler room for the core contributors to feel they were part of something that now had a genuine link to power. The Blue Labour label might not have been their choosing, but there was interest in it, and that could be useful. One man's appointment to the Lords was – for better or worse – one group's ascendency.

From early 2011 to the middle of June, this group held a series of meetings in Portcullis House in Westminster. They were not strictly formalised – they were not part of a think tank, nor did they have a strict set of members or an agenda – but they were not informal either. Glasman was the central player here, having independent relationships with all of the participants outside of the room. Marc Stears, the politics professor and college friend of Ed Miliband, would meet with Glasman once a week to discuss ideas, either in Oxford or in London. The *Soundings Journal* editor Jonathan Rutherford would visit Glasman on a weekly basis, some-times coming around to his home. Alongside these attend-ants was Jon Wilson, the academic from Kings College and – the most politically significant participant – the MP Jon Cruddas. Cruddas was the only representative of the parlia-mentary party in the room, and would suffer some of the worst conseequences from Glasman's media outbursts. James Purnell was invited but couldn't make it. David Miliband did not attend.

There were only two new players in the room that hadn't contributed to *The Labour Tradition*. The first was Duncan Weldon, an economist at the Trades Union Congress who Glasman had met when giving a talk to Crouch End Labour party. Weldon had also attended previous seminars organised by Rutherford under the latter's New Political Economy Network, an informal group of academics, politicians and journalists that had been debating economic alternatives after the financial crisis. But the first time Weldon met Glasman the pair hit it off immediately, not least because Weldon seemed to have a great appreciation for the German social economy model that was so close to Glasman's heart. Weldon had taken to coming to the Lords once a week on Thursdays – curry night in the Lords – and Glasman quickly came to see him as very influential in leading the development of Blue Labour's political economy. It was an incredibly quick ascension given that the pair only met in 2011, but Weldon remembers being taken by Glasman from their first meeting:

> I thought he was being very brave standing in the middle of a room, in Crouch End talking to a disproportionately middle class North London Labour Party audience and telling us what was wrong with the Labour party, so I sort of agreed with him and said I think the problem is a lot of the people in this room basically if they had their ideal manifesto it would appeal to people who liked *The Killing*, watched a lot of BBC4 and voted Yes to AV and with that we probably would win

Brighton, Oxford, Cambridge, maybe some of the nicer bits of Manchester and central London but there was no real appeal to that in the country, so that was our bonding and I went out to have a cigarette afterwards and discovered Maurice was also a smoker which instantly raised him up in my estimation, and mine in his, so we had a brief chat outside the meeting and he headed off. A couple of days later I wrote a blog post for Labour List which opened with some fairly stretched analogy between Blue Labour and the music of PJ Harvey from that a sense of melancholy and appeal to Old England and from that I ended up getting an email from Maurice who I went to meet and since then I see Maurice once or twice a week for the past few months

The second new player attending the meetings in Portcullis was 23-year-old Patrick Macfarlane. Macfarlane was a politically engaged Oxbridge graduate who had become interested in Blue Labour after listening to a BBC Radio 4 documentary about Glasman's ideas. Although he liked what he heard, Macfarlane said his chief problem with Blue Labour seemed to be its exclusivity; the proponents might be talking about reconnecting with people, but the ideas themselves were only being discussed by a small circle. In an attempt to rectify this, Macfarlane autonomously set up a new Blue Labour blog, and contacted Glasman about it soon afterwards. Macfarlane said that he found Glasman eccentric, but warmed to him. Looking back on their first meeting Macfarlane said: "People in politics tend to hedge things. Glasman can be a bit wild, but I like that." It is notable that both of the new additions in the room had less political influence, but were strictly loyal to Glasman. Unlike the others, they lacked independent relationships with the other Blue Labour contributors in the room.

With less of a political stake in the meetings than the other attendants, Macfarlane was well placed to describe what happened at Portcullis House. According to the group's youngest member, the participants would meet on a near weekly basis between mid-February and June 2011. They would gather after work at a seminar room in the parliament building at 7pm. Rutherford later said that he deliberately didn't want to meet in the House of Lords next door where Glasman was based; there was obviously a desire to make this more than "Glasman's board". According to several sources in the room, part of the meetings would be devoted to discussing ideas, political news and how Ed was doing and part of it to administrative issues like the blog. But by far the biggest point of the meeting was spent discussing Blue Labour's media profile. Rutherford later acknowledged that the chief point of these meetings became nothing less than "brand management", as described here by Macfarlane:

> They were meeting to discuss the brand and how it was going. They would talk outside of that too. They'd talk on the phone all the time. They were in constant communication. There was always a feeling that Maurice had more publicity. Jon could have got more of a platform but he had to be very careful.

Macfarlane said that the atmosphere at the meetings was generally good-natured, especially in the beginning. The group was informal. In a rather ambiguous space, the group were friends with shared politics as well as colleagues. But there were two problems that started causing tensions, and both centred around Glasman. The first was that although this was supposed to be a shared project amongst intellectual equals, Glasman had a higher media profile than the others, and therefore had a disproportionate influence over Blue Labour's public image. This wouldn't have been too much of a problem if Glasman didn't have a habit of playing controversial. As an organiser he was used to agitating; his words were used to excite an emotional reaction and get people talking – they never made headlines. Now that he was a Lord, the press pored over his every word. Very quickly Glasman's friends at Portcullis found they were tied to comments they not only couldn't control, but often vehemently disagreed with.

Media Storm

The first big controversy came in April when the *Daily Mail* ran an interview with Glasman on immigration. Running next to a large picture of Ed Miliband, the *Mail* reported the following quotes from Glasman that suggested Labour "lied" on immigration:

> "What you have with immigration is the idea that people should travel all over the world in search of higher-paying jobs, often to undercut existing workforces, and somehow in the Labour party we got into a position that that was a good thing.
>
> "Now obviously it undermines solidarity, it undermines relationships, and in the scale that it's been going on in England, it can undermine the possibility of politics entirely."

Glasman rather naively thought that no one would pick up on these remarks, and even if they did, he thought his record of working with migrant communities would stop him from being portrayed as reactionary. He failed to make clear to the journalist that for him, the other side of the coin to limiting immigration was granting amnesty to the thousands of illegal migrants in the country and ending child detention – policies he had actively campaigned for at Citizens UK. Glasman knew he made a mistake when he received a personal phone call from Ed Miliband. According to Glasman's report of the conversation, the Labour leader objected to his claim that the party had lied about immigration, but was "sweet" about the mistake. Apparently, Ed Miliband was "encouraging" about the prospect of more nuanced interviews in the future. His colleagues at Portcullis were less understanding. As Cruddas put it:

> His [Glasman's] way of doing it was let's say create some controversy and let's go and kick up a bit of dust which is fine, I think you need to do that occasionally, but you don't do it around simply a race to the bottom on some really dangerous terrain you know?

The problem was that Glasman didn't seem to learn from the outbursts. Less than a week after the *Daily Mail* article appeared in April, another interview for Progress – the political organisation representing the more Blairite wing of the Labour party – produced another ripple of discontent throughout the ranks. The key line that came out of this interview was Glasman's assertion that Labour should talk to the far right group, the English Defence League (EDL). The party's stance on the EDL had always been one of active disassociation, and many high profile Labour members

– including Jon Cruddas – were involved in campaigning to brand the organisation as racist and make sure it was given no platform. So when the new Lord came out and said that progressives should recognise their "responsibility" for the rise of the far right, Glasman caused quite a stir. Even more controversial was his comment that Labour should adapt their policies to speak to the EDL's concerns:

> [We need] to build a party that brokers a common good, that involves those people who support the EDL within our party. Not dominant in the party, not setting the tone of the party, but just a reconnection with those people that we can represent a better life for them, because that's what they want.'

Comments like these left his friends at Portcullis feeling hopelessly tied to an agenda they never formally signed up to and couldn't define. Although Glasman said he tried to "share out" the media appearances as much as possible, the media were reluctant to accept substitutes for his prestigious title and colourful character. They might have spoken to Cruddas, but the MP was more reluctant to be publicly involved in the project. So although the Portcullis group benefited from having a high-profile advocate for some ideas they believed in, they also felt they had no real say about how their project was exploding in the media. Towards the end it became clear that the only real control the group had was constraining Glasman's appearances, and they actively asked him to stop giving interviews. As Macfarlane describes:

> At the last meetings there was a consensus that Blue Labour had grown and got more attention than they ever anticipated

and they felt this was a bit of a challenge. They wanted to know what Maurice was doing and whether he had any media appearances… they'd ask and say "what are you doing" and he'd say "this" and then pause and say "… and this… ahem". He did tend to drip feed information.

There was clearly a fundamental split in the room. From Glasman's perspective, he wanted to push the Blue Labour brand as hard as it would go. This was more influence than he had ever had before, and he wanted to keep using it. Although he acknowledged that some of his more controversial comments were the result of inexperience, the fundamental goal of generating heat was a strategy he subscribed to. There is no doubt that he defiantly believed some version of the controversial pronouncements he was making but, more significantly, he believed you should embrace conflict rather than shut it down. So although Glasman would apologise to keep up his relationships with those at Portcullis House, he would simultaneously keep pushing the strategy he believed in.

Meanwhile on the other side of the room there was much more caution. Rutherford was the most vocal in his opposition to Glasman's approach. A truly conservative actor who was used to moving with consideration, Rutherford argued for a smaller and more strategic public profile for Glasman and Blue Labour. Explosive issues like immigration were risky topics to be treated with caution; not rocks to be hurled to crack open a debate. What was worse – Rutherford later said he openly warned in Portcullis House – was that Glasman's outbursts could actually be undermining the ideas themselves. Certainly they were already damaging the relationships in the room. Throughout the spring the controversial media appearances kept on rolling, causing greater and greater friction with his more moderate friends. Glasman said he was turning down appearances, but his profile was still rising rapidly. The media invites seemed to take on their own momentum as other politicians began to publicly criticise his outspoken views and media outlets invited him back in the hope of further flamboyant debates. Rutherford later said that he felt things were getting out of control:

When did the media start playing such a big role in the meetings?

There wasn't a particular point but the media started to take a whole new role in it to the point when it was defining what was going on, and we didn't take back that control. It got to the point when media was defining the agenda too much.

Macfarlane said that you were meeting weekly from February. Is this true? What was the point of those meetings?

They were weekly but they didn't last very long... They were an attempt to work out a strategy – what we were doing and why. In the end it was really about trying to rein in Maurice and his media interviews. So the break that happened a week ago [mid July 2011] was really a while in its coming. It was really about what our strategy was. People talk about a Blue Labour movement but there was no money or organisation... It was ad hoc, so what were we going to do? In the end it came down to what we are not going to do. The media controversies were shutting down dialogue and openness. The [Oxford] Seminars were about coalition and open dialogue, now it was whether you were for or against Blue Labour and that's not what the intention had been. There weren't that many. They were mostly me telling Maurice that something really had to stop. They weren't held in the Lords. I personally did not want that.

How did Glasman respond to your pleas to stop?

You'll have to ask Maurice how he reacted. At the time he heard and he didn't hear. But you'll have to ask him.

Why did you keep going to the meetings?

There was never a time when I officially joined "Blue Labour" – it was just something that happened. I found myself part of Blue Labour, and it was creating a huge interest, so I thought let's try and work with it. But it proved hopeless and it was soon obvious that it was not going to work as a collective. We were a very eclectic group of people. There were different groups involved but what was coming through [in the press] was a quite simplistic view – it was presented as a traditionalist, communitarian project when actually we were more open minded and more nuanced. So the thing is immigration when Jon [Cruddas] and I put something on Comment is Free we tried to think through it carefully and then it blew up in our face because of what Maurice said about it. The point was to think carefully and to keep open the paradoxical politics. There's no organisation, logic or idiom behind it, nothing pushing behind it in a strategic way into the future. It was an intervention… People [in Portcullis] all had jobs, there was no money behind it – it was all done in our spare time.

When did you get to hear about Maurice's media appearances?

Usually a short time before when it was too late to do anything about it. This was part of the so-called "brand management" – we were trying to say "no more appearances", not "what's next?" It seemed the best strategy by that time.

Do you see any advantages in the brand?

Yeah of course. Having a brand is a way of giving focus to something. Without it it will be harder to communicate the politics. But we just didn't manage it properly.

Any disadvantages?

It was Maurice's idea and Maurice determined what it was. It was becoming a caricature of itself. Maurice's provocations were contributing to that as well. It was losing diversity; it was no longer paradoxical and it was becoming counter-productive. You can't be part of something when someone is just making things up on the hoof and saying they don't believe in Keynes or no immigration. You have to have some say in the process. When things are being done every which way it's just impossible to develop it. Some of the issues we were taking are huge issues in the country that Labour has to get to grips with but you have to think it through carefully how you have that debate because an issue like immigration can become toxic. At some point you have to take it on but you have to reach the point when you can do so in a productive and strategic way.

Have you spoken to Maurice since he has been away?

Yes we've spoken and met together. We're still friends. What I've said to you I've said to him and more.

Although less publicly outspoken, the turmoil for Jon Cruddas was particularly acute. The only elected official in the room, he had more of a public profile to watch than the academics. For a long time Cruddas had argued that Labour had lost its emotional connection with working class communities. In his constituency in the East End, former Labour voters were already turning to the BNP and the EDL. But now Glasman seemed to be going too far. Cruddas was worried about the reaction from his parliamentary colleagues, many of whom came from the left, liberal, egalitarian side of the party and were strongly against any perceived xeno-phobia. Cruddas had also done a lot of campaigning against far right groups with the organisation Searchlight. These anti-racist organisations had a fundamentally different attitude to dealing with groups like the EDL. The Hope Not Hate campaign in particular had dismissed the EDL as violent thugs to be given No Platform; now Glasman was saying that Labour should adapt its policies to speak to these constituen-cies. Reflecting on the media outbursts some months later, Cruddas seemed to lament the damage Glasman was doing to the ideas behind Blue Labour as much as his personal reputation:

> it's fair to say it was a process of crisis management rather than developing a brand, it was press driven, the worst elements of it were press driven, whereas the really interesting elements of

it were contained in the ebook that was done, some of that stuff was really interesting, it was deeper, more profound philosophically very interesting, but the headlines that it garnered were counterproductive in terms of building a radical political project. So that is the brittleness of it.

Glasman personally called and apologised to members of the Portcullis group, particularly Cruddas, who he had always held in high esteem. But talking to the new peer later, it was obvious that he felt the mistakes were not just the result of his personal naivety, but also a rather "ungenerous" media industry that was intent on shutting down debate:

I think they [the Portcullis group] found it difficult to be part of something that they couldn't define publicly?

To which my gentle response is I've always tried to share... I gave Marc radio invitations, newspaper pieces, Jonathan too, and Jon Wilson. Two things, I guess, the first is that there wasn't the same level of interest in those but that was something that will change in time as people discover their abilities, but the second thing is I really had no idea in retrospect how big it was getting and I was really not, I didn't you know, with you it's nice to meet people and talk to them, with the chat with Mary [Riddell], I didn't even remember talking about immigration it was an academic chat about what could be done.

Do you think you made mistakes with journalists?

Yes. The first most important mistake I made was what I call conversational arrogance, I forgot who I was talking to, to journalists, thought I was having a chat, the second was not making the conscious transition from sort of academic and not local organiser to national political figure, the third was not concentrating on always giving the paradoxical balance, so the thing I regret most of all with the Mary interview was to talk about immigration which is necessary but not to stress the legal, you know the regularisation of illegal immigrants.

Why didn't you talk about your work with migrant communities?

given my life [I thought] no one would question it, it's the same with feminism, if you look at my life that's the life, I've always been committed to women's power, particularly low paid women, with immigrants I've always worked with immigrant communities intensely so, so I was the last person in the world I thought who would be accused of sexism and racism, I really thought that couldn't happen to me, my response was oh my God, the bad thing was I relished it in a way, fuck you if that's what you think, that's not what it's about, it's the way you get, the way I would think the liberal progressive elite demonised people so quickly and I thought that was impossible to do that to me but I learned.

Labour vs Labour

In June Blue Labour started receiving attention from women

and the feminist movement. Labour MP for Bishop Auckland, Helen Goodman, had read *The Labour Tradition*, and found it highly offensive. She wrote an extensive pamphlet on the subject, published on the political blog *Liberal Conspiracy*, and appeared on *Newsnight* to debate the issue with Glasman head to head. The transcript between the two Labour members came across as rather divisive:

GOODMAN: It is quite anti-women, there are essays in [*The Labour Tradition*] that blame the breakdown in social order on the independence of women. I think most women are quite pleased we've got an equal pay act.

PAXMAN: You also suggest it is jingoistic.

GOODMAN: It is jingoistic, not Maurice but one of the other authors, there's a sentence that says the social disorder has been caused by the loss of men's entitlement, as if white men were entitled to the fruits of black people in the colonies and the exploitation that went on in the colonies. I mean this is an extraordinary document.

GLASMAN: Well I think this is all a little ungenerous. There are a variety of voices in the book. I think the idea that this is anti-women is just wrong.

Here was one trait about Blue Labour that the media loved: it pitted members of the same party against each other. Such heated internal debate made great TV. But of course – partly for the same reason – it could cause serious damage to the reputation of the party. One tangible example of this was Glasman's appearance on Sky News' Murnaghan programme in early July alongside female Labour MPs Caroline Flint and Diane Abbott. Flint had always been sympathetic to Glasman's ideas, but Abbott objected in the strongest possible terms. The MP for Hackney started by saying that by choosing immigration as a "signature issue", Blue Labour was in danger of "perpetuating myths". The sight of three high-profile Labour members arguing so heatedly on live TV – and disagreeing on Labour's record on migration in office – did not look good. The Sky debate crossed the line. Abbott later received a phone call from Labour's head press office asking why they hadn't known about the appearance.

But senior figures in Ed Miliband's office never seemed as angry as they might have been about such publicity. In an interesting display of what appeared to be a more open culture under Ed Miliband, his office remained remarkably soft on Glasman. Although it would be wrong to over-exaggerate the impact of this – the reaction might have been very different if Glasman was a member of the shadow cabinet, and punishing someone for talking about immigration would not have been a strategic move – Wood insisted this was something they were not prepared to do on the basis of principle rather than pragmatism:

> If you are true to your word about having a vigorous debate about principles and directions of travel as a party, you have to be prepared to allow disagreements to take place inside the party such as the one we've seen around Blue Labour.

This approach was later acknowledged by Ed Miliband himself. At the end of the summer in which Glasman had consistently made controversial headlines, the Labour leader seemed surprisingly understanding and sympathetic to his newly chosen peer. In marked contrast to Gordon Brown's leadership style, Ed Miliband acknowledged that moving into public life was a "difficult journey" for anyone, and didn't seem to regret his decision to make Glasman a lord. In fact, he portrayed it as an intentional commitment to openness that he wanted to characterise his leadership and distinguish him from his predecessors:

> I think Maurice is a very important voice for bringing new issues to the table, I don't agree with lots of what he says, he doesn't agree with some of what he said as far as I can tell! That is what happens, but you know Maurice is not a politician, he's someone who I thought, which is why I made him a peer, I thought he had something interesting to say about the future of the Labour party, and you know the point about this is that it's sort of my approach that is you have to give some intellectual space for some people, for a long time people felt there was a line and you had to toe the line and there wasn't any space to deviate from that line, this is about saying actually there is space for debate.

Ripple effect

Although Ed Miliband's office might have granted Glasman sanction in what they regarded as a generous experiment in Labour party openness, the old guard were less amused. Glasman's outbursts were obviously witnessed by other party members who clearly didn't share his views, or want their party to be associated with them. The deputy leader of the party Harriet Harman – who Glasman once said "embodied everything that was wrong" with the modern Labour party – had started asking questions about Ed Miliband's relationship with Glasman. A longstanding advocate for women's rights, Harman would certainly be receptive to any concerns members raised about Blue Labour's attitude towards women. Alongside these questions, the leader's office said they also received complaints from a couple of MPs, including Roy Hattersley.

If Blue Labour was causing controversy in the parliamentary Labour party, it was also rippling out into the wider constituency parties. Adam Bartlett, a Labour activist in Slough and self-declared fan of Blue Labour, witnessed high-profile members of the party being actively hostile to the Blue Labour agenda. More than that, he argued that these figures were misrepresenting the philosophy itself and "misleading" the leadership about the reaction Blue Labour was getting from members. Bartlett emailed this experience with his MP Fiona McTaggart and the two guest speakers Ann Black, chair of the National Executive Committee and Martin Phillips from the South East Policy Forum:

> Fiona and Martin both mentioned BL several times and you could see in their faces and from their tone of voice that they absolutely hated it. It was introduced as a copy of "Big Society", promoting small government and also pandering to "racists in chip shops". When folk asked more about it Martin told us his opinion that BL only gained traction as Lord Glasman is a mate of Ed's. He talked about the pro-patriotism aspect and specifically the promotion of taking pride in St George's flag as though those things are self evidently evil.
>
> Thankfully just about everyone at the meeting seemed non nonplussed. They mentioned tighter immigration policies and one of the Asians present said she shared concerns about

immigration being too high. (A common view from Asians in Slough – the polls that suggest a majority of first and second generation immigrants favour tighter controls seem to be correct – just read about this from the "In Defence of Maurice Glasman" article).

... At the very end of the meeting Fiona seemed to misrepresent the criticism of Ed as criticism of Blue Labour even though at best only three (of sixteen) had seemed to even partly share her and Martin's dislike... for someone so clearly dedicated to serving the public to hate blue labour so much suggested the battle would be very challenging.

The snap

Events came to a head on July 18th when Glasman made the front page of the *Telegraph*. The broadsheet's journalist Mary Riddell had picked up on another interview that Glasman had given to the Fabian Society on immigration. In this interview Riddell reported him calling for a renegotiation of the European Union's rules on migration. Glasman's comments would have caused controversy in the Conservative party, let alone the Labour party:

> Britain is not an outpost of the UN. We have to put the people in this country first.

Riddell then asked if that meant stopping immigration completely for a period:

> Yes. I would add that we should be more generous and friendly

in receiving those [few] who are needed. To be more generous, we have to draw the line.

Ridell then asked Glasman if he had any sympathy with Iain Duncan Smith's controversial call for British jobs for British workers:

Completely. The people who live here are the highest priority. We've got to listen and be with them. They're in the right place – it's us who are not.

Glasman's comments made the splash in the *Telegraph*, and then hit the tabloids soon after. But it was not the article itself that presented the real threat to Blue Labour; it was the damage it did to Glasman's relationships.

This was the turning point for the Portcullis group. Cruddas was furious. Rutherford was incensed. The private discontent in the room could no longer be contained; the pair felt it was necessary to publicly distance themselves from Glasman and the Blue Labour project. Two days after the *Telegraph* article was published, an article appeared on the *New Statesman* website pronouncing Blue Labour "dead":

Blue Labour, the informal Labour policy group established by Ed Miliband advisor Maurice Glasman, is to be effectively disbanded.

Labour MP Jon Cruddas and Middlesex University academic Jonathan Rutherford have both informed Lord Glasman they no longer wish to be associated with the project following an interview given by the controversial peer in which he expressed a belief that immigration to the UK should be completely halted.

A third influential supporter, Dr Marc Stears, is said by friends to be "deeply distressed" by Glasman's comments, and is also considering his future engagement with Blue Labour.

It was a harsh piece. Although Rutherford and Cruddas later reflected that the headline had been somewhat drastic, it did reflect a genuine anger on behalf of the group. There was no one – not even Glasman – who was prepared to stick by the comments. Stears, always one of the most dedicated supporters of Glasman and the Blue Labour brand, publicly said the group had appeared to "implode". Wilson, the academic from Kings, said the comments were "frustrating", and described the future of Blue Labour as "uncertain". Anthony Painter, a friend of many in the Portcullis circle who had contributed to *The Labour Tradition* ebook, wrote an article for the *Guardian* condemning Glasman's comments as "toxic". Glasman was isolated.

This then was a real existential threat to Blue Labour, and Glasman knew it. He openly acknowledged that he had "really fucked up". He stopped checking his emails and refrained from typing his name into Google "for sheer mental health reasons". Although the project had been more than one man and a brand, it was now threatening to become just that. In July, Glasman said he had to "make a call" about how necessary it was to have certain members on board. He was building new alliances – like Weldon and Macfarlane – who were more loyal to the Blue Labour brand than his older friends, but they had less political clout. What was clear was that Glasman didn't want to let the brand go. In the week the

New Statesman pronounced his movement dead, he said he wanted to "go on building alliances and relationships".

It was at this point that Glasman went on holiday. He disappeared for a fortnight to Sicily with his family, and spent some time reflecting. Although his absence was noted amongst his friends, it wasn't noticed on a wider political stage because it coincided with the summer recess. Almost everyone went away. Although Glasman did refrain from making any more controversial comments, he did not leave the media entirely. An article appeared in the *New Statesman* making a public apology for his comments. In a true Glasman display of openness and emotion, he pleaded forgiveness for what he described as his "crassness and thoughtlessness" over the past few months. In the same piece he pledged a "vow of silence over the summer". Not only did that raise eyebrows amongst those who wondered what would happen in the autumn, it also wasn't entirely accurate. Aside from being interviewed for this book, Glasman spent a good part of his holiday on the phone to Weldon, who remained faithful to the Blue Labour camp. Together they put together an article on political economy recommendations for Ed Miliband that was then published in the Financial Times. Although not explicitly billed as a Blue Labour article, it did refer to the philosophy, and called for many of the things Glasman had already asked for under his brand – including regional banks, workers representation and interest rate caps.

By the summer of 2011, it was obvious that Glasman had shown a high level of naiveté on the public stage. He had come a long way from the East End where he spent years working as a relatively anonymous academic doing community organising, and he was taking time to adapt. Political skill did not come automatically with political appointment.

But an obituary for Blue Labour would seem premature. When Glasman returned from holiday he made peace with his alliances. Although one of the most angry at Glasman, Cruddas said he was still prepared to be associated with the label. Stears was quoted in the *New Statesman* as a "Blue Labour thinker" without objection and the relationships with Ed Miliband's office remained intact. Later it emerged that throughout the summer, Glasman was attending meetings in Portcullis House with Ed Miliband and his senior leadership team. Those links were not going to go away. In the Conclusion we will hear from Ed Miliband and David Miliband about just how influential those ideas continue to be. The brand may have been dented, but the force of the personalities and the strength of the ideas mean that Glasman's influence is unlikely to disappear. It may be the end of a chapter, but not a story. Blue Labour, by influence if not by brand, lives on.

Conclusion

It is barely eighteen months since Glasman first uttered the term "Blue Labour" in the wake of his mother's death. In that time the phrase had risen from a personal moment between a man and his wife in their living room to a set of ideas that are being debated in the national press and referenced by the leader of the country's formal opposition. In the summer of 2011, Blue Labour had been through the full arc of publicity. It had risen quickly to prominence; now it was threatening to fade away. After Glasman's controversial outbursts on migration and the EDL, the media pronounced the movement dead in July. But it is the contention of this book that Blue Labour ideas will not disappear. Although there is now a legitimate debate being held about whether the label "Blue Labour" is still helpful or a toxic brand worth abandoning, the fundamental ideas that the agenda embodies remain powerful. The philosophy's key principles are still being debated in important circles, the personalities remain colourful and dynamic and the relationships between its top supporters are – if somewhat bruised – still going. Blue Labour has sparked an interest that is likely to continue having influence under Ed's leadership.

Early signs suggest that this is already the case. A few

weeks before Ed Miliband opened his first party conference as Labour leader, he proposed that the party should reform clause one of the party's founding constitution to put community organising "at Labour's heart". In a formal recognition of the work of his older brother, Ed Miliband also called on conference delegates to allow the Movement for Change to formally affiliate to the party. It was a magnanimous gesture, given that the Movement for Change had originally started as a rival campaign to distinguish David Miliband as a better candidate for leader. This was particularly true given that David Miliband had remained personally involved in the Movement for Change since he lost the leadership, devoting his time to ensuring it had the funding it needed to carry on. In an echo of what was already outlined in this book's introduction, Blue Labour ideas were bringing together a pair of brothers that were split by the leadership campaign. Despite Ed Miliband's label as a Brownite and his older brother's label as a Blairite, they were now united on the community organising agenda first introduced to them by Glasman. The proposals might not have been Blue Labour in brand, but they were Blue Labour in spirit.

Certainly Glasman does not want to abandon the brand or the ideas. In fact he has been taking active steps to make Blue Labour stronger. At the time of writing, Glasman is pulling together a new advisory board of Blue Labour players to help direct and refine what he wants to see as a growing movement within Labour. It remains unclear whether Blue Labour under this governance will remain a public brand or simply seek private influence, but either way, the evidence suggests it will continue to shape Labour.

Blue Labour has already had a significant and underplayed

influence on the ideas at the top of the party. This book has documented how through little more than an uncanny ability to build relationships, Glasman made his way into the heart of David Miliband's leadership campaign, building the original alliances necessary for the introduction of the Movement for Change. He did all this whilst maintaining connections with Ed Miliband, helping the younger brother develop his pledge on the living wage. Even before the leadership battle, this little-known academic had helped Ed Miliband develop Labour's ideas for the 2010 election and penned a speech for the former prime minister Gordon Brown. This influence has largely been informal, working through contacts rather than any institutional position or accountable set of channels, and it has perhaps been stronger because of it. Unelected players like Marc Stears and Stewart Wood are good friends with Ed Miliband, and continue to push a number of Blue Labour ideas – although they often left out references to the brand – in rooms where the decisions get made. Blue Labour has always been testament to the power of relationships; it is perhaps no coincidence that the proponents' influence continues to be built on it.

But if Blue Labour's networks are important, so are its ideas. Its analysis has struck a chord in the party. It has succeeded in articulating a critique of the previous Labour government that many share. The belief that New Labour grew too close to the City and failed to achieve balanced growth is widely held. After three terms in office, the need to look for answers to social problems beyond the market and the state is widely acknowledged. As Ed Miliband himself wrote in the forward to *The Labour Tradition*, "It is our families, friends and the places in which we live that give us our sense of belonging". The feeling that Labour become administrative, elitist and technocratic in office is widely acknowledged to be one reason why they were voted out of office. Blue Labour's call to fundamentally change the language and character of the party is provoking a response. The fact that Blue Labour calls for the party's regeneration to be built on a revival of Labour's history and tradition – rather than as a strategic response to the poll date of the day – gives it moral legitimacy. Even where Blue Labour's relationships have broken down – as with David Miliband – the ideas and their influence have lived on.

This final chapter, written on the eve of the 2011 party conference and Ed Miliband's first anniversary as leader, will examine what resources and influence Blue Labour has to make these changes in the wake of the media storm. In tune with Blue Labour philosophy, it will ground that analysis in the relationships that the proponents still have, looking first at its connections with Ed Miliband's office, then working out to other potential Blue Labour leaders, the parliamentary Labour party and the party membership. Finally it will turn to the electorate, examining whether Blue Labour ideas could achieve results for Labour at the polls. It is the central contention of this chapter that although Blue Labour has a set of powerful and influential relationships at the top, they are about quality rather than quantity. Blue Labour might be calling for a revival of Labour's traditional working-class roots, but at present it remains a set of ideas amongst a middle-class, political elite. Whether that can be changed with initiatives like the reformation of clause one remains to be seen.

How Blue is Ed Miliband?

In an interview for this book after the media storm engulfing Blue Labour, Ed Miliband said that he continued to draw inspiration from its agenda. Although he voiced his usual reservations with Blue Labour's attitude towards the state and distanced himself from Glasman's recent controversial comments on immigration, it's clear that the key messages continue to stick with the leader. Ed Miliband said that, for him, one of the most useful ideas to come out of Blue Labour is that there is "more to life than the bottom line":

> I think Blue Labour is directing us towards values and insti-
> tutions and things that we didn't talk about enough when
> we were in government... I've said New Labour rebuilt the
> fabric, but didn't do enough to change the ethic, this ethic of
> your society then that takes you to the kind of institutions of
> your society, so you know, do you just care about your local
> football club or the way the football clubs are run based on
> money or is there more to it than that, do you care about your
> high street just being available to the highest bidder, what are
> the institutions you value, do they matter beyond the bottom
> line.

After the controversy surrounding Glasman, it would have been easy to keep these ideas but distance them from the Blue Labour brand. But the Labour leader was not doing that. Instead, he said he wasn't going to disown Glasman over the comments made in the press to date and openly credited the ideas associated with the brand for feeding into his new emphasis on responsibility:

vibrant movements produce successful ideas, movements that have the unity of sort of you know not allowing debate, dissent, it's not the way our democracy works, so why should it be the way the Labour party works? I'm pretty clear about the direction I think is important and Blue Labour ideas, and responsibility is an important part of that, but you know, I think it's important for the party that the debates can go on.

Although Glasman's personal relationship with Ed Miliband is often overplayed, his more significant relationships are rarely covered. It is interesting that for a philosophy that is so focused on community, its key power relationships remain with players at the top of the party rather than the bottom. Glasman describes his relationship with the leadership as "good and constructive" and casually estimates that he meets someone in Ed Miliband's office about once a week, although there is clearly more correspondence by email and phone. Every six weeks, Glasman is invited to a three-hour discussion about policy and strategy at the leader's home in a meeting for "friends of Ed". He is on first name terms with senior members of the leader's office. Lord Wood, Ed Miliband's strategy adviser who was widely credited as one of the people who helped get the new leader elected, has a close friendship with Glasman and celebrated his birthday with him this year during a conference in Berlin. Tom Baldwin, the leader's head of communications, comes to visit Glasman in the Lords. Glasman knows Greg Beales and Lucy Powell, referencing their interests and backgrounds. Although some of these relationships are less favourable – Glasman never mentions Polly Billington – the links are well established. Glasman likes the culture of Ed Miliband's office, saying it has "roots in the non-liberal elite". By this he means that many of the key players might have been to Oxbridge, but like him, Marc Stears and other Blue Labour proponents, they were often educated in state schools.

The results of Blue Labour's relationships are already making themselves felt in Labour's style and policy. Ed Miliband's reform of clause one is just one aspect of this. According to Cruddas, a series of meetings were held in the leader's office in Portcullis House where he, Glasman and others discussed Blue Labour ideas over the summer of 2011. Although not explicitly billed as "Blue Labour" meetings, they involved discussions about many of its themes, including family and community. Most recently in the wake of the scandal engulfing News Corporation – the global media empire that was forced to close one of its major newspapers after it illegally hacked phones for stories – Ed Miliband gave a speech on responsibility that was said to be strongly influenced by Blue Labour ideals. In this address Ed Miliband called for everyone in society to take responsibility, linking what happened at the top of a giant company with the MPs expenses scandal of 2009 and the financial crisis of 2008. In a move that irritated certain members of the parliamentary party, Ed Miliband also linked the theme of responsibility to those members at the opposite end of the power spectrum, saying that those committing benefit fraud should also take responsibility for their actions. Outside of Ed Miliband's continued commit-ment to the living wage and initiatives like community land trusts that have been influenced by Glasman and Citizens UK, Ed Miliband has also been considering wider policy ideas influenced by Blue Labour. The idea of putting workers on the remuneration boards of banks to safeguard against overinflated bonuses has been discussed in senior circles.

More widely, Blue Labour might be having some impact on the culture of the Labour party under Ed Miliband. In the autumn of 2011, the founder of the Industrial Areas Foundation Arnie Graf – who has something of a mythical status amongst community organisers in the UK after being trained by their hero Saul Alinsky – is returning to work with the party's new general secretary Ian McNicoll on changing the culture of the party. His links with Citizens UK make him particularly interested in developing the ideas piloted by Movement for Change. Graf has long acted as an informal mentor for Glasman, and it was through him that he met the Labour leader.

When it comes to community organising then, Glasman believes Ed Miliband is "beginning to get it". The Labour leader has been known to quote Alinsky and rearrange the chairs in community meetings so that members of the party and the public sit in a circle together rather than separated by a podium. The leader found this approach particularly helpful when he went to visit community groups after riots engulfed the country in the summer of 2011. In a sign of Ed Miliband's new-found respect for Alinsky's ideas, he even took Graf to his local Labour party. The leader later said he was impressed with the practical change Graf helped initiate there:

> one of the things he [Graf] said to my local party it's such an important point he said look every new member of the Labour party should get a visit from someone (preferably someone they would like to see again) you know, because relationships precede action, if you just send out a newsletter saying there is

a meeting at 8pm, in the village hall next Tuesday it's not the same as building relationships and that's so important thinking about the way political parties work and it sort of gets away from some of this "minutes of the last meeting" culture.

Experiences like this may well be informing Ed Miliband's support for changes like the reform of clause one. It is a line of thinking that brings him closer to his brother. In a sign of both Milibands' ability to put their commitment to the party above personal history, Ed Miliband formalised the experiment started by his brother, and David Miliband was gracious in his response. Even before the official news about clause one reached the press, the older brother said:

It's very good that the party leadership has embraced these ideas and supported them. That gives people confidence about the party culture from the top.

Blue Labour players

There is no doubt that Glasman wants Blue Labour to be a serious political project. He wants the brand to continue and its influence to increase and he is taking steps to achieve those objectives. Although he says he doesn't want to be tied down by launching a think tank, he is putting more formal structures in place. A number of anonymous donors – the most influential Glasman says doesn't want to be named – means that he now has a five-figure donation to put towards his project. He has already started renting his own office in Dalston and hired an assistant, Dan Leighton, who used to work at the think tank Demos. Glasman believes that these resources will provide a base to build the brand and perhaps write a book:

> I would love to see Blue Labour having really dissolved in to the Labour mainstream, become the Labour mainstream that in five years I would love to see a genuinely united party around the ideas of redistributing power to regions, to cities, to the workforce, to the common good, to all areas of life, to genuinely engaging with the areas that confront us, how do we build relationships under conditions of financial domination and to reconstitute relational power in association as the driving force of democratic change... I'd like to see this generate new and surprising relationships between divided forces you know, so left and right, old and new have gone, old is not available and shouldn't be the new is really tired and has been... well the banking crisis and the lack of transformational welfare.

Although Glasman is still the key proponent of Blue Labour, others are heavily involved. Glasman recognises the danger of appearing like a one-man band and is working on building more Blue Labour leaders. He is also setting up an advisory board around Blue Labour to build alliances. Not a public group, the aim would be to help generate broader support around Glasman's project and prevent him from making the mistakes that he has made in the past. Glasman was still discussing this idea at the time of writing, but he was not presumptuous about who might appear on the board. He expressed a hope that his original friends would want to be included, referencing Jon Cruddas, James Purnell,

Marc Stears, Duncan Weldon and Carole Stone of market research company YouGovStone. On top of that Glasman is anxious to seek more representation from community and faith groups:

> It's [the board] not a public group... it's got to be involving labour unions, women, Muslims, the representatives or leaders of the different groups they have got to do the work and one of the crucial areas that is always missing is a genuine Muslim leader... That's where I am at, so far I've been dancing away but it's time to reconstitute relationships that matter.

Winning hearts and minds: the party

Glasman is open about the fact that Blue Labour's alliances are weakest in the parliamentary party and the old Labour guard. The former business secretary Peter Mandelson has publicly criticised Blue Labour's "populist, anti–immigrant, Europhobic, anti–globalisation language". Tony Blair said that the party wouldn't win by indulging in Blue Labour's "nostalgia". On the other end of the party's political spectrum, MPs like Diane Abbott and Helen Goodman have criticised Glasman for being sexist, xenophobic and unsympathetic to benefit recipients and the vulnerable. There are also criticisms from parliamentarians including Roy Hattersley about Blue Labour's anti-liberal streak. Although Blue Labour does have some alliances in the parliamentary party – most notably Blairite MPs Tessa Jowell, Hazel Blears and Caroline Flint – there is a question about whether any Brownite MPs have come on board. Although Ed Miliband is normally associated with this wing of the party, influential players like Ed Balls and Yvette Cooper are completely absent from Blue Labour's story. It is only Glasman's close relationships with the leader that enables him to overcome anonymity and hostility in the wider party.

Outside of the parliamentary party, influential leaders in Labour remain dubious of Glasman's unpredictability. This threatened to undermine important bases of support for Blue Labour. Will Straw, fellow at the influential think tank IPPR and son of the former minister Jack Straw, is a friend of Glasman. Straw says he is interested in Glasman's ideas, particularly on community organising and the need to reinvigorate party structures. He also has some sympathy for Glasman's critique of Labour's "technocratic and managerial" approach. However, he believes the term "Blue Labour" is not a helpful one given its reference to conservatism. Indeed in the wake of Glasman's media crisis, he believes it is now a "duff brand":

> I felt let down, as a Labour party activist who considers Maurice a friend and who is sympathetic to many of his ideas, that he would be so careless in putting forward a set of propositions that were badly thought out and would inevitably cause a backlash – not only against him but against the broader set of ideas that he and others had been advocating. This gave those who were critical of other parts of Blue Labour the opportunity to throw the baby out with the bath water. When the storm over immigration broke, I felt disappointed that he hadn't learnt from the backlash following his comments about the EDL. He should have realised that following his ennoblement and with the title of "Ed's guru"

he had a responsibility to be more careful about the language that he used.

How deeply Blue Labour can embed itself within the party will depend on whether Glasman can build a broader set of alliances within it. This in turn will depend on whether there is a genuine appetite for change amongst influential Labour players and the parliamentary party. Those who subscribe to Blue Labour tend to be frustrated and angry with the party's status quo. This is what leads them to call for genuine root and branch reform within the party, from culture and policy to organisation and language. But it is an open question how many other MPs believe that this is necessary or desirable. The MP who has been most heavily involved in advocating Blue Labour ideas, Jon Cruddas, certainly does feel the need for radical change, but he does not occupy a formal position of influence in the party, and he is the first to acknowledge that his ideas are far from representative of the Parliamentary Labour Party. In fact according to Cruddas, some of his colleagues have already tried to shut down the debate:

Did members of the parliamentary party raise objections about Blue Labour?

Yes, yes, pretty much everywhere I think, you see it all depends how you treat the situation Labour has faced in the last couple of years, I would say it hasn't got any intellectual vitality around it, people don't know what it means either to be Labour so you know when people say it's not like the early 80's when Labour was at each others' throats, I would say yes, but, that seems to me to be a sign of torpor rather than vitality, so say there is no discussion and that is a virtue does not necessarily help Labour get out of the hole it is in which is arguably one of the greatest crises it has ever had as a political party. So the key is to create discussion and create a bit of controversy and try to import a bit of vitality intellectually to define what it is, if I don't know what it [Blue Labour] is as a Labour MP I tentatively suppose a lot of people out in the country don't know what it stands for but that's not, so to me the way it was defined as something which was whatever people wanted it to be was a sign of people's lack of intellectual confidence in that they were just denying discussion, that was something that was an attempt to stimulate discussion, nothing more than that actually, it wasn't prescriptive, it wasn't programmatic, it wasn't, and that's why I don't think you can define it, I know that works against the project in one sense, but you know.

Do you think the rest of the party was deliberately shutting down the debate?

it was subject to continuous caricature functionally by the people who didn't want to get out from under their own liberalism and identity politics more often.

Would you be willing to be publicly involved in Blue Labour now?

Yes... hmmm, yes... Arguably we're in a worse position empirically than we were in 1983 and 1931, so we have to put some jump leads on it, you have to stimulate a bit of discussion, and since the election, the first parliamentary Labour election I went to the basic tenor from everyone who spoke was well if we just clamp down a bit on welfare cheats then get a bit harsher around our immigration story then we could be back in, in a bit and I was like fuck that, you know? It doesn't really work for me. So if the alternative option is to support a bit of a discussion that creates a bit of heat and opposition around the parliamentary Labour party that's a price worth paying.

Is there a critical mass of MPs who think there is a crisis of identity at the moment?

I don't see a lot of evidence of that no. I think the general consensus seems to be that we are doing well. In the parliamentary party.

Does Blue Labour need to pin down its programme?

Yes. Well, maybe it's performed its task, and maybe what you don't want it to be is prescriptive, programmatic, because that is when you get into trouble because the troubles come when policies, because the danger for Labour is not policy, it's that you know, like setting up twenty nine policy review groups is not the solution for Labour's crisis I would suggest, so you know the remedies are not policy ones, they are much more fundamental ones with character.

How much does Ed Miliband's office listen to Glasman?

Well, they listen to him a lot and Maurice likes that entire power gig. So it works well, look.

Do you think Ed Miliband's office would do well to listen more to Blue Labour?

Yes. I guess, I mean, the danger is, you do a speech on responsibility one month and you then do one on education, it's, there is a danger of seeing these as discrete things, what you need to do is get a kernel, a philosophy together and then use it when you talk about everything as your fundamental political project and story, narrative, whatever you want to call it and that's where the speech on responsibility first time I thought he [Ed Miliband] began to do that. The question is whether that is something he just does relentlessly for three years, or whether he thinks he has done it when he writes a speech on it.

Where does Blue Labour go from here?

So, you know, will it be seen as a sort of bodged up series of discussions or will it have a longer lifespan I don't know really, it all depends on how he [Glasman] wants to play it I think. If he just wants to go around shouting look at me, I can do blah, blah, blah he will get gunned down again but if it becomes more rigorous and less you know press driven, that's where its virtues will lie.

Winning hearts and minds: the members

Glasman has been keen to build alliances around Blue Labour. To that effect, he has been visiting a large number of constituency parties to explain his ideas, frequently speaking at more than one meeting per week. Interestingly it is often the most critical, liberal constituency parties that are most interested in hearing his ideas, and he has had a warm response both at Crouch End and in Southwark, if only because of what one member referred to as his "strangely refreshing character".

In particular, Glasman appears to have attracted a following of young Labour men writing in support of his ideas. As well as Patrick Macfarlane, the young blogger who autonomously set up the independent Blue Labour blog, an independent party member from outside London, Joe Sarling, said he was taking it upon himself to push for Blue Labour ideas in the West Midlands. Adam Bartlett – a young activist in Slough – also wrote to say he was "totally in love with it". Paul Bickley, senior researcher at Theos – a think tank focusing on religion and public life – is excited that Blue Labour "opens the way for a significant re-engagement of religious traditions within the Labour movement". For some members of this demographic at least, Blue Labour seems to be tapping in to something they have felt for a long time but have not been able to express. It is interesting however that their love of Blue Labour is also connected to an isolation within their own local parties, raising questions about just how deep this feeling goes. One Labour activist based in Southwark said he was happy to call himself Blue Labour, although he didn't want to be publicly named here for work reasons:

Would you consider yourself Blue Labour?

I have always been Blue Labour, it's just no one had a name for it and left me feeling sometimes a little isolated because you would meet perfectly normal party members who believed all those things but then you would go and spend time with Labour students, the young Fabians and on the internet and it would appear that nobody believed those things and politics was about something completely other than what you had grown up believing that it was about.

How does Blue Labour fit with your politics?

I'm left wing but I'm not progressive, I don't think change is good in itself I want things to get better, not just different, and quite often I think it was at its worst in the Blair era we found ourselves in an attitude where if things were different it meant they were better rather than having an honest conversation about how they were genuinely improved. The other big thing is that Labour did lose its place as an organisation in communities, it might have been Phil Woolas who said the problem in 1997 was anyone who had done any thinking started running things and stopped thinking. It's an interesting point anyway, but it's not just the thinking we stopped doing it was in large engaging and party members were treated as a leaflet delivery mechanism and leaflet delivery is very important but it's not the be all and end all.

Do other Labour members you know feel the same?

I don't know. It's what I am, there's no shame in it. I would call myself it because I have no personal political ambitions. If I wanted to be an MP I'd probably stop calling myself it, which is a bit of an issue isn't it? Because the party members don't like it, largely they don't like something they think it is but isn't. When you are off having quite a shallow "please support me in this election" meeting you don't want to have an ideological argument.

What about the country as a whole?

I think it fills a fundamental gap in the market and appeals to people who weren't voting or voting for people other than Labour.

Movement for Change

True to his word, David Miliband remained committed to the Movement for Change long after the leadership campaign. He helped secure the organisation funding from Lord Sainsbury to continue training Labour activists, and continued to personally attend training events, visiting one event in the North East just a few weeks before the 2011 party conference. At this time, David Miliband was optimistic about the future of the organisation he helped create:

> The first thing to say about Movement for Change is that it is really just getting going. We trained 1,000 people during the leadership campaign. But that was really just a test. We now have a proper national organisation, independent of the party but supported by the party leadership... It's a young institution with, I think, sustainability and durability as well as excitement and novelty.
>
> We plan to train 10 000 community leaders over four years. It [the Movement for Change] can contribute four things. Firstly, new skills. Secondly, it can turn the party outwards.

Thirdly, it can help spread best practice and finally it can honour an important part of Labour history that has been buried a lot. In other words it can reconnect a party that doesn't nurture its roots in the community.

Although David Miliband remains a trustee on the Movement for Change, the organisation is now headed by Blair McDougall, a longstanding Labour activist who worked on David Miliband's campaign. Presiding over a team of five in an office in Brixton, McDougall's mission is now to train 10,000 community activists before the next election. Although he has never worked for Citizens UK, McDougall and his team received training at the organisation before they launched in 2011. He also maintains a friendship with Glasman.

McDougall believes there are a number of important reasons why the Movement for Change will remain important for Labour. He stresses its importance for reinvigorating party membership. In an electorate of some 45 million, a total Labour party membership of 200,000 is worryingly low and there is a feeling that local parties will need to offer a more rewarding experience if membership numbers are going to rise. On a deeper level, McDougall believes that reconnecting with grassroots communities can help Labour become a better party more grounded in the experiences of people outside of Westminster and Whitehall. This is a belief shared with proponents of Blue Labour, who have always seen the rejuvenation of the grassroots of the party as essential part of reinvigorating Labour's character, style, leadership and policy substance. Although the Movement for Change does not accept the Blue Labour label or any other political badge beyond Labour, McDougall seems to recognise this point:

> in politics now you need an authentic voice and you can get an authentic voice, we had one in 1997 I felt but that was almost handed to us by a really angry electorate who were ready for change and to find that authentic voice again, we're either going to have to wait for that to happen again or we're going to have to do an awful lot of hard work to really understand people's lives, because I don't think we do.

It is important not to over-exaggerate this commitment to openness and party democracy. Ed Miliband's office might have talked about the urgent need to regenerate the party, but how deeply it is committed to this goal – which is shared by many sections of the party including Blue Labour thinkers – remains open. Groups such as Compass and the independent blog LabourList have argued that the recent Refounding Labour consultation – a project led by Peter Hain about the future of party organisation and democracy – has still not gone far enough. Before the announcement of the reforms to clause one, Cruddas said he was afraid Refounding Labour was "dribbling into nothing".

There are also internal splits about exactly how party democracy should be achieved. A number of groups within Labour argue that the party needs to connect with communities and rejuvenate its base, but not all of these groups believe that the methods Blue Labour advocates are the best means of achieving this. For Blue Labour, reconstituting local parties means learning from the Citizens UK model of community organising, which is grounded in Saul Alinsky's understanding of power and the importance of relationships. David Miliband's Movement for Change campaign demonstrated that there are real issues about transferring that community model to a political party. Meanwhile other groups are pioneering different models of community engagement that seem to be working well. Caroline Badley, campaign co-ordinator in Birmingham Edgbaston, pursues a model of "community campaigning" for example. Closer to traditional party campaigning methods, Badley has run petitions and collected signatures to achieve change and build networks. Similarly, the anti-racist organisation Hope Not Hate – a group that Cruddas is heavily involved in – was widely felt to have done good work running single issue campaigns against far right groups such as the BNP and the EDL in areas like Barking and Dagenham. Some party activists have expressed concerns that, through Glasman, the Labour leadership has understood party renewal in one narrow way, when actually these other methods are worth learning from. As Anthony Painter, political writer and commentator who contributed to *The Labour Tradition*, says:

I think the problem with going back to Blue Labour is it emphasised one of those models… a lot of game-changing good that was done by other techniques… that led to against the wave electoral and local success have been sidelined as a result, and so I think to go back to your question I think Ed, I think he gets it in general terms, I don't think he gets it at the detailed level and at the detailed level what you have to do is let three flowers or five flowers or ten flowers bloom… and we're just going for the London Citizens/Movement for

Change play, never been proven in a party setting – esoteric to say the least.

… I'm not knocking London Citizens in terms of what it does as it's clearly had major successes; I don't think its relationship with the Labour party has been properly thought through.

When this concern was put to David Miliband he said:

We're not simply importing the Alinsky model, we're learning from what we've always done in this country – our history based on relationships, trust and mutuality. This is a British as well as an American tradition. It [the Movement for Change] is not a substitute but a supplement for renewing and supporting an effective party that will bring us closer to the country.

Blue Labour votes

Blue Labour is concerned with the haemorrhaging of working class votes from the Labour party. The statistics suggest that it is a justified concern. Some four million working-class voters have deserted Labour since 1997, compared to 1.5 million middle-class voters who also stopped voting for the party during the same time. But research and opinion is still divided on how Blue Labour politics might play out at the polls. For all its talk of reconnecting with communities, the project remains largely based in Westminster. The Blue Labour brand is discussed almost exclusively amongst the political and academic elite. People may argue that Blue Labour is characterised by a populist streak, but it is certainly not the result of a populist movement or an uprising on behalf of conservative working-class Labour members. Even Labour's chief institutional link to working people – the unions – remains disengaged from this debate. In the summer of 2011, Ed Miliband himself acknowledged that, "most people don't know about Blue Labour".

But the fact that working-class organisers aren't leading the charge for Blue Labour does not necessarily mean that the changes it calls for would play badly with this demographic. Blue Labour's premise, after all, is that many voters are disengaged and excluded from Labour politics. It's difficult to expect these same individuals to believe they can come in and influence the agenda. The best answer, then, is to look at the data.

Two pieces of research suggest that Blue Labour might be able to re-engage its working-class base. The first is from the Campaign Company, a communications consultancy that uses the British Values Survey to understand the psychology of the British population. Focus groups and values surveys conducted over the last two years find Britain to be socially conservative on most issues, and conclude that Labour's biggest challenge is to reconnect with Britain on social affairs – principally welfare, immigration and crime – rather than on the economy. Interestingly, reconnecting on these topics is much more about changing the language that Labour uses rather than the specific policies the party proposes. Consistent with the Fear and Hope report, this piece of research found that there was a core demographic known as "Settlers" that Labour's rhetoric is simply not appealing to, and that they were in danger of shifting their support to the far right. Although there is a danger of isolating liberal middle-class Labour voters by becoming more conservative, Nick Pecorelli, associate director of The Campaign Company, explains that there is a significant chunk of the population which currently feels ignored by the party:

> A core of the electorate – around a third – are Settlers, this group can be found in any class and in rural, urban and suburban areas, but the biggest single group is in the working class. They are the most anxious about immigration, identity, fear of crime and making ends meet. They are often nostalgic for a time when Britain was better. This means they typically believe the best solutions stem from the past – bring back matron or teach history in schools are the kind of things that appeal to them.
>
> … Labour has to work particularly hard at getting the Settlers back because they are less engaged than the other segments – Pioneers and Prospectors. This can only by a combination of tackling head-on the belief that Labour no longer understands them or shares their values and this means talking about the way of life issues in the right way and returning to these themes repeatedly. It also means old-fashioned pavement politics as there is no substitute for face to face contact with Settlers.

The second piece of research is the Fear and Hope survey commissioned by the Searchlight Educational Trust in early 2011. This attitudinal survey asked over 5,000 people what their views were on English identity, faith and race. The researchers, Nick Lowles and Anthony Painter, concluded that there is "not a progressive majority in society", and that there was a widespread fear of "the other". In particular, there was a clear correlation between economic pessimism and negative views on immigration. The survey found that there are six identity "tribes" in Britain ranging from "confident multiculturalists" to those who were most disaffected – the "active enmity" group. But it was the new centre ground in this newly identified spectrum – the "cultural integrationists" who are motivated by authority and the "identity ambivalents" who are concerned about their economic and social security – who are most of interest to Blue Labour. Together they make up 52% of the British population. Although Painter does not believe that Blue Labour has all the answers, he does argue that these groups could respond well to a resurgence of conservative thinking in the Labour party:

> the key group for Labour is actually the "identity ambivalents." No political party manages to speak effectively to them. It's Labour territory but Labour has decreasingly been able to communicate to that group… The problem is that Blue Labour misses them too as it speaks to a world which is not really their reality. It feels like the urban version of shire Red Toryism speaking to "cultural integrationists" – here the Conservatives are already strong. Some conservative themes could potentially speak to these voters but we're not talking the "traditional working-class" in modern gear here.

Others share this concern that Blue Labour might not be able to speak to the demographic it claims to represent. Phillip Blond of the think tank ResPublica, for example, argues that Blue Labour's appeal to the working class cannot work because Britons no longer label themselves in that way. They are too aspirational, which means the brand won't appeal to them. It is worth keeping in mind that over a third of Britain's school leavers now go on to university, and with manufacturing industries still largely in decline, there is less respect associated with the working class label. Blue Labour, says Blond, hasn't really caught up with this:

> [Blue Labour] hasn't really recognised what Blair was writing about and speaking to, Blue Labour still won't appeal to the majority of British people, it still remains an appeal to a type of working class that is very much in the minority, that's unionised, and low waged, there is no appeal here to small business people, or workers who wish to be high wage and high skill,no appeal to the modern structures that most people live in or desire .

Even if voters did accept Blue Labour labels, Blond does not believe that Labour would ever be able to swallow the socially conservative values it proposes:

> I think Labour will always be hostile to social conservatism, or as I term it "social conservation", it will always privilege Liberal autonomy above all things, so I never think it can be a radical party for that reason.

Although Blond does not rate Blue Labour's ideas as they stand now, he does think they are underestimated by his colleagues in the Conservative party. Blond says that although current cabinet members do have Blue Labour "on the radar" they are not worried that it will steal capital C Conservative voters. This, Blond believes, could be a mistake:

> I think they underestimate him [Glasman] and Ed Miliband,

but if Ed keeps with the notion of squeezed middle, transmutes Blue Labour into that space and I think that's a potent mix.

Future

Blue Labour is still young. At the time of writing, it is barely eighteen months old. Similarly, Ed Miliband has not yet been elected a year and he is still defining his policy platform and approach as Labour leader. Critics argue that he is presiding over an intellectual vacuum in the party but – old or new – there are still significant interests competing for Ed Miliband's attention. From the left, the Red Book is on the verge of being published. Written by a collection of authors under the new left group within Labour known as GEER, the aim is to combat what it calls the "neo-liberal" strand of thinking in the party. A rejection of free market economics, it has less to say about the changing role of the state. On the other side of the debate, the Purple Book is simultaneously being released by the New Labour pressure group Progress. With contributions from the likes of Peter Mandelson, Frank Field and Alan Milburn, the book looks at the non-statist traditions within Labour, but has less to say about a change in attitude towards the market.

As the closing lines of this book are being written, Blue Labour is also vying for Ed Miliband's attention. Taking something from Red and Purple, it challenges the new leader to take on both the market and the state and reinvigorate Labour's sense of community. Although the brand is newer than the rest, its call is based on traditions that are immutable and values that are timeless. The fundamental worth of this philosophy is left for the reader to judge, but few would deny that it offers an original contribution to the debate. It is also hard to question its energy. Already Glasman is preparing for party conference where he has a packed line-up. He will have to run from room to room with ideas that are likely to continue causing agitation and appreciation. It is still hard to predict which emotion will win out. Blue Labour has caused serious tension, but its central ideas have also succeeded in uniting two brothers supposedly split along traditional Brown-Blair lines, making them speak with one voice after a difficult and emotional campaign. They both endorse the need to build relationships and institutions to combat the forces of the market and to some extent the state, as well as an urgent need to reinvigorate the party through community organising. Whatever chord Blue Labour has struck, it is still ringing. It remains to be seen how far the leader will listen, and how much the rest of the country will choose to hear.

For more information, resources and to comment visit
tangledupinblue.co.uk

Rowenna Davis is a journalist and has written for the *Guardian*, *Independent* and *New Statesman*, specialising in social and political affairs. A Labour councillor in Southwark, she is a longstanding charity and community activist.

Steve Richards is chief political commentator for the *Independent*, author of 'Whatever It Takes' and presenter of BBC Radio 4's 'Week in Westminster' and 'The Brown Years'.

The Unfinished Revolution

Chaos

The Plot Against the NHS

The People's Book